THREADS

THREADS

A BOOK OF PRAYERS AND STORIES

BY

ROSS MACKENZIE

Introduction by Barbara Brown Taylor

Illustrations by Judith Olson Gregory

All profits from the sale of this book will be used to advance the work of the Abrahamic Initiative. The Initiative, founded at the Chautauqua Institution, New York, in 2000, seeks to bring Jews, Christians and Muslims together to work on issues in ethics, the arts, and factors making for a civil society.

Published 2001 by Chautauqua Institution

Inquiries should be addressed to
Chautauqua Institution
P.O. Box 28
Chautauqua, NY 14722

05 04 03 02 01   5 4 3 2 1

Printed in the United States of America on acid-free paper

To all those
who find it very hard to pray
but very easy to tell and listen to stories

CONTENTS

INTRODUCTION

P ublic prayer comes in so many different forms
that it is difficult to say one true thing about
all of them. Depending on who you are and where
you live, there are prayers around the dinner table,
prayers at the state legislature, and prayers at the
annual Chamber of Commerce banquet. Even in
churches, the variety is staggering.

In some places, public prayers are read from
books. This has the advantage of linking those who
pray them across centuries and continents. It also
keeps leaders from inserting too much of them-

selves. In other place, prayers are composed for the particular occasion at hand. This has the advantage of stirring those who pray them with fresh language that speaks to the present moment. It also keeps leaders from inserting too little of themselves,

In every case, the marvel of public prayer is how it travels in two directions at once. Addressed to God, prayer addresses the congregation as well. We learn what we believe as we listen to ourselves speak to God. We learn what we want as we listen to what we ask, and quite often we find that securing the desires of our own hearts becomes less important than seeking the desires of God's heart. Good prayers teach us how to pray.

They also teach us what it means to be a community, as we practice the plural pronoun that makes us all kin. In common prayer, our "we" will stretch as far as we will let it. It is big enough to include those who are absent as well as those who are present. It is big enough to include those who do not believe as well as those who do. It is big enough to include the living and the dead. Good prayers address God on behalf of all humanity.

In order to sound true both to God and to the congregation, these "we" prayers are unstintingly honest. They tell the truth about what it means to be human, ignoring neither the awful parts nor the glorious ones. They tell the truth about the world, and especially about those regions most in need of redemption. Above all, they tell the truth about God, without saying more than God has said or promising more than God has promised. Good prayers are honest.

Since so much truth tends to be unbearable, it helps if public prayers are also exquisite. It is amazing how much truth the human ear can admit, if the language is right. For this reason, the best prayers tend to sound like poems, in which every word reaches as high as words can go and then stops, catapulting listeners into the presence of the One beyond words. Good prayers are beautiful.

Ross Mackenzie does all things well. Shaped by ancient traditions of prayers read from books, he has become a writer of public prayers himself. He writes like someone who has prayed enough to know where the quicksand is. He writes from and for the community of faith, with concern for those far beyond its bounds. When he says "we," he means everyone. Even someone who reads this book alone on a desert island will be folded into the family of God. Ross tells the truth, and he tells it so exquisitely that it is impossible not to listen.

We do not listen to him, however. His prayers are so powerful because he manages to get out of the way. He has an uncanny ability to know both what we need to say and what we need to hear. While the language is entirely his, he gives it away for free. By the time he is finished finding the right words, most of us are convinced that they are our words, not his.

This volume is reason for celebration. It is a book of common prayer for any community that is lacking one, written by one of God's own poets. Ross Mackenzie's prayers do the one true thing that all public prayers are meant to do: they set us on the path to God, urging us onward without ever once getting in our way.

Barbara Brown Taylor
Clarkesville, Georgia

PARADISE IN
ALL ITS BEAUTY

Space by itself has no existence unless there is light. Light makes each thing we see alive and present to us. Light is therefore a sign that the Divine is present and near us, for God is Light. Light makes God's presence real to us in particular locations.

On the first day of creation, according to the Scriptures, a joyful hymn broke out: *Let there be light.* God "speaks" in the beginning not in words but through light. Perhaps we should speak about the Big Light rather than the Big Bang. For the light that shone on that long-distant paradise still shines in every part of the natural world. The beauty of the world is an image through which we can hear God speak to us, not in words but in light. When we understand that God's light is in everything we see or enjoy in nature, at once the long-distant paradise will appear again in all its beauty.

The journey of the soul to God begins when we listen to the word God speaks in nature. So place yourself imaginatively now in the fairest point you know. It could be a garden, an island, a mountain or a desert. . . . or in some of the places that follow.

But watch for the thorns and sharp stones. They can wound. But we need them too.

This Fair Point

Father of Light and Mother of our Souls:
there was music in this place long before we came,
when the birds sang and the waves broke softly on the beach.
You spoke your words here long before anyone of us heard.

And the song lingers.

In this fair garden of the soul
we who are lovers of song, and speech, and dance
have come with gifts of praise and gratitude.

Breathe your own life into us,
Warm us with your light,
that we may glimpse your own unchanging beauty
surrounding us in every growth and form around.

Breathe your own life into us
and warm us with your light again and again.
For you have placed us in this fair point of your creation
to care for it, and make it fit
for the Messiah to come home to.

Lord of the Summer Season

Lord of each summer season,
when flower and field and fruit unfurl their ribbons to the skies,
smile on us in this holy day
set apart for our rest and refreshment.

The morning is yours,
rising to its fullness;
eternity is yours,
angling down into every place and time.

Mother and Creator of hill and valley, wind, and the song of birds—
all are yours.
And gladly we live
in this garden of your loveliness.

But nothing in the world is sufficient for our need;
for even in its beauty shadows of decay bear down on us;
even in the garden the wounding thorn can pierce and bloody us.

Creation is not nurse adequate to bind our wounds,
nor friend enough to console us
when we are weary and full of care;
nor rescuer enough to lift us
when we're low and lost;
nor counselor enough to heal us
when we are in despair.

Abuse, betrayal, cruelty,
where are the tears for the pains we cause?
Gossip, hate, and insult,
what bitter fruits are rooted in our souls!
Neglect, oppression, and unkindness,

where is our peace of heart?
Violence and hatred of the stranger,
do we really mean to make you sad?
How can sin and grace dwell in the same heart,
as if we had two different hearts?

For all we have done in error and confusion of mind,
forgiving God, forgive us.
Take the things that bring us down and keep us low,
absolve, annul, forgive,
and draw their sting and hurt from them.
This will be your renewal of us,
thus will we rise with the morning into fullness.
Thus by your release we will be free,
and gain again the mastery of ourselves.

You have given us the visible world
as a gift earmarked for us.
Help us, then, to see that this world of beauty
is nothing other than the place to love you,
Maker, Poet, and Modeler,
whose dream became our actual world.

Day Is Dying in the West

The twilight here is grey and pink and green.
The lake is still;
and to your right, behind you,
a plum is setting, not our customary sun.

The lake is still. . . . And

heav'n is touching earth with rest.

The plum Sun God is trailed
by scarlet, green, and honey wheels. . . . And

the deepening shadows fall.

Night's dark grave has covered now
the corpse of the plum Sun God.
And the lake and my heart
are still and cold.

Who will lighten this darkness,
lighten our darkness? . . . So

lighten our darkness, we beseech Thee . . . .

The lake is still.
No light or life can burst
from the waters of this womb.
Ripples and waves refract no honey, or green, or red now. . . . But

love can carry us to God. So

from another place
where you least expect it
another kind of day will come.
And you shall be warmed by the dawn of this fair point,
grey, and pink, and green.

Light Falls, Does It Not?

Light falls, does it not—
   or breaks? Why should it not
    blossom like a tree?

Standing in the Need of Prayer

This is a story about a divorced Protestant, a Muslim, eighteen illiterate, undis-ciplined children, and a Catholic monk: not a bad mix of how God works in many disguises.

The divorcee is named Janice, age (I am being less than discreet) 40; her lover, Sammy, 54; and the children from the project, 12-14.

The children had been—not to put too fine a point on it—dragged from the city project to the confirmation class of a downtown church. Poor, hungry, disorganized, and from broken homes, they knew adults, for the most part, as self-centered, unloving, and undependable.

Janice had the task of giving them religious instruction prior to con-firmation. She sat down and pondered three questions: First, what is non-negotiable in teaching religious faith? Second, how do you com-municate that with a minimal use of words? And, third, how do you con-vince a white, middle-class religious education committee that there is more than one way to skin a catechumen?

So (such are the workings of the providence that shapes our ends) now we can add Islamic inventiveness to Protestant perplexity. Sammy had seen a Roman Catholic priory in St Louis. He suggested a field trip.

Thus, eighteen children showed up on the appointed day, permis-sion slips in hand. The kids were rowdy outside the starkly beautiful building, with its fluted roof that touched the ground in twenty places. As they entered, a hush came over them. Father Simeon, in monk's robe and with English accent and a new beard, spoke with them. His lov-ing warmth put them at ease. He asked for questions, and they sur-prised Janice by asking real questions about the life of monks, the things in the sanctuary, and the priory school. He invited them to look around. They did, and then scattered.

The prior is spacious, maybe a hundred feet across, with the altar in the middle. All around are sculptures and statues, done in powerful con-temporary form. Janice, sensitive that the monks might have strong feel-ings Roman Catholics about holy things, asked Simeon if there was any-thing he would rather they did not touch He said, No, except he would rather they didn't fool with the candles. The candles were on holders from one to three feet high, some flickering brightly before a centuries-old wooden statue of the Virgin Mary, with a semi-circular kneeling rail outside. Janice ends her story.

> So I kept an eye out for the children as they neared the candles. But no need to. A kneeling-rail is for kneeling, and, as they came close, they all kneeled down. And as Sammy and I watched from across the sanctuary, the strains of, "It's me, it's me, it's me, O Lord, standing in the need of prayer," came from the children, picked up and lifted high by the mystical acoustics of the domed roof. The sound lingered, the candles brightened, and I knew something I hadn't known before. I have no words for it. It's something like keeping alive a sense of mystery and wonder. It's almost like tasting the holy.

We Ache to Possess

We ache to possess
the rare and perfect faith of simple souls,
the wisdom of the pure in heart,
who let us see that even a shadow is witness to the sun;
that all twists and turns of human life
are waves of a divine purpose.

Love, who are our blessing,
you are our book, our guide, our understanding.
You are our thought and our heart,
our wounds and healing.

Help us, then, to see you present in everything,
every moment a taste of the holy.

Then, since you exist in all things,
One and Simple God,
anything that happens to us,
inwardly or outwardly,
will reveal some new intent you have for us.
What more can we ask?
Where else need we look?
What else hear,
but the inner Voice that speaks continually to our hearts?

A Call to a New and Blessed Service

Compared to those who worshiped here, age upon age ago,
with drafty walls sufficient for the divine indwelling,
we're rich as Rockefeller now.
So much will now be required of us.

Measure us, then, Creator God,
by how well we have crafted our life of faith
and formed our personal character
in the workshop of your world.

Give us eyes to see each natural thing
as bearer of your light,
all living beings
as bearers of your image.
Help us turn our torn and suffering body politic
towards life not death.
Give us wisdom to make the service of others
pattern of the coming age.

Worker God, weaving what your word had spun,
you planned creation,
breaking the silence with your birthing song.
When the first hymn rang out in the heavens,
"Let there be light,"
you were pleased to make a home place for yourself on earth.
Don't leave us now,
but stay with us awhile.
Make us more often mindful
that you never leave us ever.

For all gifts of color, rhythm, sound, and movement we bless you,
and ask that they may turn us to ponder your glory.

For all varieties of speech and language we bless you,
and ask that they may enrich our mind,
redeeming the waste of a tawdry culture.

We commit ourselves now to you,
and offer you a people's reverent response:
to see if we can envision the world
as best of all possible worlds
It still is the day the Lord has made.
The day has come,
day of remembering,
day when faith sets us on another journey,
day of joy and happiness,
day to sing,
day to give thanks,
day to join the beginning
of a season of renewal.

On That Mountain

The Feast of the Transfiguration celebrates the occasion when Jesus took Peter and James and John, and went up on a mountain to pray. While he was praying, the appearance of his face changed, and his clothes became dazzling white.

On that mountain they let their eyes roam at you, Jesus,
and realized their eyes were melting.
It all became too piercing bright for them to see you,
and the edge that divided you from the surrounding universe
changed into a layer of vibration from which all limit was lost.

And there was no boundary between heaven and earth.

Here in this clearing of a primeval forest
people like us have turned great clods of earth,
and planted, and built, and formed a place
where only a veil, thin as gossamer, separates heaven from earth:
and families gather in the rooms of their childhood,
and strangers speak kindly to strangers;
and dance, and harmony, and speech
bring us a beauty that is healing.
Through the veil of such lesser beauties
we glimpse the luminous simplicity of your own true beauty.
Here and now it reaches into the very depths of our being,
so that our whole selves surge.

What else is there to do but say we love you?
What else is there to do but sing in explosive bliss,
Holy, holy, holy?

On a lonely mountain
you had a glory in your bosom that transfigures—

the dazzling brightness of the Creator
who set the whole universe vibrating with a nod, saying,
Let it be.
On the mount of your transfiguration,
you said,
Let it be again.

Let the divine image in each and all be free from tarnish,
the burden of human sorrow and suffering be lifted.
Let neither death nor darkness ever extinguish the light of your life.
What else is there to do but offer ourselves to you,
here in this place, one by one?
How else can we respond but asking only
that your love may shine in all we do or say?
So, then, may the world come to see that you are its true light,
guiding creation to its perfect end.

GOD NOT
SOMEWHERE ELSE,
BUT HERE

We experience God as the encompassing Spirit when we become aware that we (and everything that is) are in God. We always do so either in memory of an event or in the midst of an experience. In both, we are in the presence of the holy.

When we understand this, we will see how limited a view of the holy we have so far possessed. "In the beginning," we read, "the Spirit of God swept over the face of the waters." Then the word came, and billions of years passed in the twinkling of an eye, and Bingo! a creature with a DNA pretty close to ours stood up and walked the surface of the earth.

From Spirit to matter, shimmering on one side and clay-like on the other, the holy is in and under every *thing*. In and under every *one*. We know we are in the presence of the holy not only in the pulsing of electromagnetic waves but in the self-balancing biped that makes fire, makes love and makes something as beautiful as a Parthenon or a Shakespearean sonnet. We know we are in the presence of the holy not only in the organization of the molecules that create a baby but in the disorganization of the molecules that mark our death. And at every place we can sing our song, Alleluia, alleluia, alleluia.

Everything Is Beautiful

Since time's beginning,
and Adam was still between water and clay,
all your works *have* praised your name on earth, in sky, and sea,
and everything is beautiful.

What works, dear God, are yours; what fitting praise attends them:
quasars in the distance, furnaced with energy beyond our calculation;
quarks everywhere, tiny beyond our capacity to measure;
wild roses interweaving honeysuckle like fingers of child and mother;
birds singing of a love we never shall decode;
rains falling in darkness, bright with fresh noise;
lake waters, beckoning, haunting as a prayer room.

Everything is beautiful.
And who has made it all, the old saint asked,
but unchangeable Beauty.

Yourself.

The Stage Manager

All backstage activities occur at the cue of the stage manager. Lights change, the curtain rises, the players begin at the nod or command of this one, who alone of all can never be seen.

When the corners of our world seem too dark to penetrate,
and confusion and loneliness lie heavy on our hearts:

> *give us the patience to wait awhile.*
> *Change the light for us.*
> *Bring on the figure that we do not yet know,*
> *who is waiting for your cue.*

When we swear there's only cosmic silence,
and we puzzle to find the rhyme or reason for life's dissonance:

> *lift the curtain somewhere deep within us.*
> *Let us see another figure in the wings,*
> *who comes with words from you*
> *that only can be meant for us.*

When we set our face like flint against being tolerant and loving—
No thanks.
We've been down that road before.
We've been hurt before.
We remember the pain,
and want no more of it:

> *give us the confidence that on cue*
> *someone to whom you give the nod*
> *will come on to show us love*
> *that never could have been imagined.*

When it seems as if our lives are a Shakespeare play,
done by a third-rate touring company.
And it's so hard to find the beauty in the muddle.
Look at it:
What should be sublime is marred and messed.
Why had we no time to rehearse this part?
Why do heroes act like fools?
Why has the sacred been made to look so seedy?
Why can we never penetrate the inner core of things?
Where has the poetry gone, the pride of character?
The curtain couldn't come down a moment too soon.

Show us that your treasure lies hidden in every field,
your beauty is for the finding in any mud or mess.
Show us—my God!—that we too have a role
in all that happens around us
(not just the walk-on part of those who simply watch and wonder,
waiting for the final curtain).

Show us what it is to have an active role,
to be actors in the dramatic work
in which you have assigned our parts
in bringing mercy, virtue, peace
to those who need and long to have
our voice, our gift, our caress.

And prompt us all again
to make each action on our part
occasion of your grace,
and answer to your cue.

The Conversion of Mrs. Brown

After the first five minutes in the company of Joyce Snell and Margaret Watson, I concluded that they were two of the dumbest girls I ever met. I use the word in both the literal and the popular sense.

When I met them, I was pastor in a vast, low-cost housing development on the fringe of a Scottish city. Before three thousand houses were dumped by builders on its fields, it had been the Buttercup Farm, with wheat growing in its fields. Joyce and Margaret were two skinny stalks in the new and living harvest that was growing among the rows of brick and concrete.

They were shy to the point of muteness, with not a word to stutter out about their work, their friends, or their interests. Together they came one spring—such are the workings of grace—"to join the church," they blushingly mumbled. Leaning against one another like those fabled Irish houses that have to be sold in pairs in case one falls down, they were received at the end of twelve long weeks of classes on the meaning of church membership, still utterly dumb.

Each fall the congregation had what we called a mission of friendship. After some minimal training, we sent members of the congregation off into the parish to visit the houses that were being opened in the rapidly expanding area. The technique was to send the visitors out in pairs—older with younger, experienced with inexperienced. Through an incredible lack of thought we never calculated that Joyce and Margaret would volunteer for parish evangelization. They did, one fall. Through an unforgivable mistake we sent them out together.

They arrived at the front door of Mrs. Brown, about whom the kindest thing that could be said was that she had probably never darkened a church door in her life. When she opened the door she saw them, one pushing the other forward, like children going for shots, each struck dumb with fear. Finally, when she could make no sense of what was going on, and assuming they were either foreigners, aliens, or refugees from the institute for deaf and dumb further up the road, she invited them in and (this being Scotland) regaled them with cups of tea. Joyce, the dumber of the two, then electrified the household by announcing, "We are the mission of friendship." That was the sum of what she could stammer out. Margaret murmured quietly: "We want to tell you about Jesus."

I guarantee that if I had gone to see Mrs. Brown, she would have resisted the blandishments of the professional clergy as she had done so well for all her life. She came to see me the following day. I chilled, waiting for the bad news. "If these two girls went through hell to tell me about Jesus. . . ." Long pause. "They didn't. But I'd like to know something more about what you're all about in that church of theirs."

Joyce and Margaret remind me of a phrase of G. K. Chesterton: "Each generation is converted by the saint who contradicts it most." In a world that is too clever by far for its own good, where victory goes to the smooth-talking politician, and the sale goes to the fast-talking, wisecracking drummer up of business, we need the sanity and sanctity of God's shy and silent ones. They may not be glib in their speech. We may judge them dull because they aren't as clever as we are. They may not be movers and shakers, but they would rather be judged dumb than have their dreams invaded by the loquacious dummies.

What weird spirit grabbed them that moment I will never know. Maybe it was God's Spirit. They stammered, and out dropped their faith. In doing so, they clarified God for me. They reminded me that there is a language of stammering that is more eloquent than the language of speech.

"I mean to deliver my people from captivity," God said to Moses on the mountain where the bush burned strangely. "My God," Moses replied, "I'm no crowd rouser." Actually, what he said was, "O my Lord, I have never been eloquent. I am slow of speech and slow of tongue." And God said, "I shall help you speak."

Praise, then, to the all stutterers who can hardly release the firmly blocked word. Praise to Moses, and praise, too, as far as I have a vote, to Peter the fisher, and Thomas Aquinas, the "dumb ox of Cologne," as he was called on account of his reticence, to Anne Frank before her captors in the concentration camp, and to the Jews of Silence in the Soviet Union. Praise to that company of the quiet and the shy anywhere who, warring against every natural instinct, bend to some inner command

and offer the most nakedly simple witness to God and to God's love, or to peace and its opportunity, or to justice and its necessity.

It is enough to know that God counts the will for the deed; enough to know that God hears the substance in our stammering, that in our silence God hears and respects what we intend.

The Eternal Lover

The Song of Songs tells of the love between God and the beloved. Can it really be—
that God loves us with a passion? Can it be that coming to God, we come to a
lover who will never let us go?

We're weary, God, of aimless search,
willing to try again the path that leads to you.
We're wanderers, begging refuge on a gloomy night,
ragtag moochers, hardly fit for decent company.

I welcome you at an open door with clasp and kiss.
I welcome you to the joy of love's renewing.

Can any love be born in us again, Eternal Love?
Can we, who fled your love, be ever welcome home?

Your absences—let something lie on them, gently now, like snow,
Let me see again how lovely you are, how much I long for you.

Do you, then, pass over the absences from you
that stare us blankly in the face?
Are you, really, the life in every breath we draw,
the pith of every desire we have,
the lure that draws us back to our only bliss and freedom?

I am yours and you are mine,
I reach for you, the one I love, with heart and soul.

Can it really be—
that a human heart can hold the infinite?
a mind like ours can bear your radiance?
If so, then soften our hearts and bathe our minds with light.

I hear your steps so clearly, for you are near now.
When love unlocks its floods, we feel no bliss so much.
We are in each other blest.

Tell us how to woo you, Love,
tell us how to woo you!
Bring us to the place, your open heart,
where you yourself become so much our own
that we lose ourselves in you, as saints have taught,
and find ourselves as we are meant to be.

When I see you turn to me, my heart stands still.
My heart stands still, and I open the door.

Teach us how to woo you, Love
For our fond hearts long only for your heart.

Sweet One, we love you,
but most because you see into our hearts,
and we become aware that your whispers to us
are dearer than a lover's voice.

Gracious One, we love you,
for to think of you is rest,
to serve you is all joy,
to feel you close is the end of all desire.

When I see you turn to me, my heart stands still.
My heart stands still, and I open the door.

EgyptAir/Icarus

On October 31, 1999, EgyptAir Flight 990 crashed into the ocean a few hours into the eleven-hour flight from New York to Cairo. As the plane entered into its last descent from 33,000 feet, the co-pilot recited a simple prayer, not once, but many times: "Tawakilt ala Allah." It means, "I put my trust in God."

In Greek mythology, Icarus was son of the inventor, Daedalus. He perished by flying too near the sun with waxen wings.

This plane I'm sitting in:
it's a clone of the one that fell
through forty seconds of terror beyond imagining,
God willing it?
Willing?
What God would will such pain?

How, then, do I make sense
of this vast space around me now—
clouds layered on clouds,
soft, like dimpled icing on a cake?
Below, the ruffled lakes bear shadow for a moment
of the wings we bear,
wings sealed by rivets firmer than any molded wax.

How can I speak of any caring God
in this blue, cold, and endless canyoned void,
birthed in the great hot cauldron
that the Scriptures call creation?
Where is the cunning Framer of a world
when death evokes such fear,
and science has no measure of our destiny,
and logic declares there is neither void nor vacuum
but simply nothing at our end?

Olympus, throne of Zeus, was far too high
to let the gods come down to speak to us,
Hades too deep by far
to let the witnesses rise from the dead
to bear their muffled testimony
that there is no sense,
no logic, plan, or meaning anywhere.
And no theology can pry a heaven open
to let us see the President of the Immortals
planning to have his sport with us.

God, cunning Framer that you are,
it takes courage I do not have
to "justify the ways of God to man."

So what is God,
but bedtime story, told
to comfort and keep safe?

But safety wasn't in the plan
when EgyptAir, Icarus of our time,
came tumbling down in mockery of human skill.
No layered, cushioning clouds that day
kept metal and flesh from their joint deadly impact
on the cruel sea.

How can I speak of any caring God?
And yet, and yet. . . .

Here in my hand I hold a weapon of resistance
against the fierce marauder doubts
that fold me in their darkness otherwise—
a pen, a former of words, that written, spoken, or sung,
will contradict the fierce illogic of my doubting.

For every word that ever can be spoken, written, sung
is word of God and word from God
and word in whom the Primal Poet speaks.
And every word that I can ever hear
from pilgrim, sage, or scientist,
is testimony that all things work
according to a perfect symmetry.

For even in that awful fall,
with forty seconds of terror beyond imagining,
the blood still coursed in vein and artery,
the heart still beat, but faster in each cardiac cycle,
the thin, moist membrane in each lung
continued the necessary exchange of oxygen and waste.
Even in the water's grave
the very fragmentation of the body parts
bore witness to a higher logic
by which the processes of life are guarded,
sacred in their beginning,
sacred in their being,
sacred in their ending.

So even at the water's grave we make our song, Alleluia, Alleluia, Alleluia.

Icarus, your seeming pride was no undoing,
but witness to the word that forms and guards and rules all
things,
and shapes a pattern that we do not see,
and only guess at in our deepest pondering.

What God would will such pain as Icarus knew
when hurtling to his water's grave?
What God will will my pain
when time and change have had their way with me?

None but the God who spoke,
when forming this vast space I see around me now,
when calling into being and cherishing
the endless, canyoned void I now can learn to call my home.

So, God of Icarus, Allah of Gamil al-Batouti,
use words like these as weapons of resistance
against the hurts and doubts that fold us in our darkness.
Use every spoken, written, singing word
of pilgrim, sage, or scientist,
to be a sign that every seeming end
is part of a new beginning,
sign that all things keep their ancient symmetry,
and every moment we are standing,
even if unaware,
at the very gate of paradise.

When Icarus fell, and saw his water's grave
opening to him from the depth below,
did he say, "Fool I was, to have taken on this journey
daring to climb to heaven"?
Or was it, "If Zeus will,
I will stake life and fortune
to see the face of God.
I put my trust in God."

So, if the end be death—
his death, or anyone's—
would not that death itself be sign
that all things work according to a perfect symmetry?

So let his prayer be mine:
"Creator God,
take praise from this and every death."
From every death an Icarus rises again
to prove that death can never say the final word.
For memory remains,
and memory binds the living to the dead,
and death has no dominion over them.
In every death a new beginning comes,
by which the processes of life are guarded still.

So God, the God of Icarus,
take praise from every downfall, every pain, and every death,
and fold them into every cell
of this vast space surrounding us,
a space that only fools call void.
We put our trust in God.

Icarus, saint that never was,
you testify to the sacredness
that fills to overflowing
every space and void that,
can I but understand it,
are body of God on earth,
and blood of the God who suffers in every fall,
but keeps the stars in their ancient courses,
and lets us wait in hope
for the word that will come
when all words have been written, and sung, and spoken,
and we have final testimony that all things work
according to a perfect symmetry.
Only a membrane faint as a cloud
can keep us from that final vision,
that ultimate discernment.

We Are Lonely

We are lonely.
God of the cold, vast universe,
We want a heart to speak to,
a heart that understands,
a breast on which to lean.
If only you would come to us.

We are scared.
God, whose name can never be adequately named,
we've cried to you from the depths,
but who has ever answered?
We want an arm to steady us from tripping,
a finger to point the way.
If only you would come to us.

We are bewildered.
God, must you answer our every question with a question?
Must our hearts forever thirst and never be filled?
Will our eyes always strain to find a glory that they can never behold?
Have you created in us a capacity that even you can never satisfy?
If only you would come to us.

Draw near, then, Comforter in our loneliness,
Guardian in our fears,
Island of sanity in our bewilderment.

Come in disguise to us,
come in surprise to us,
come as the rain to refresh us,
come as the fire to warm us.

Come as friend,
come as stranger,
come as gift or come as pain,
but come as "fount of every blessing."

For what are these longings within,
if not implanted by your own design?

What are these thirsts we feel,
if not that you have given us to taste the water of life?
What is the wonderment that comes to us,
if not that some gleam of your eternal being
has touched us in this place and time?

So we turn and return to you now,
for your perfection calls us,
your mercy bids us welcome
and your grace will not leave us in the darkness.

So we turn and return to you now,
for all our trust is in your mercy,
our final refuge in your love.

Stunning in Unchanging Beauty

You are good, God,
and you love our human kind,
stunning in your unchanging beauty,
life in our passions and passion in our lives.

What a charm it is to see the light that is beyond all light
twinkle and gleam in all created things around us.

In sand, and wind, and waves, and wings and sounds of distant storms
we find enduring joy.

In hopes that sustain us
and loves that enfold us
and songs that we sing, with voices cracked or glorious,
we taste the wine of the land of eternal youth.

In times when we are alone in the dark and tied to pain,
we feel an embrace around us that is yours,
divine and without flaw.
Now, urged by the joy and hope and love and compassion that we
have from you,
we feel the need to pray: for the world and for its peace.

Ruwanda,
Kosovo,
Chechnya:
the names of the scars
the quarreling human family bears
slip through our fingers
like knots on a bloody string.

Our eyes, seeing these beads of sorrow
begin to weep.
But your heart is big,
so come apart with us and cry with us.

Eritrea,
Ramallah,
Chiapas:
still they come,
these awful hurts
the agony, scourging and crown of thorns
thrust down on the members of our quarreling human family.

The Holocaust,
Hiroshima and Nagasaki,
Oklahoma City:
Still they come, these awful hurts,
victims crushed and
innocents abused:
these knots on the bloody strings—
our rosary of human violence
with only the sorrowful mysteries,
not glorious,
pains beyond imagination to conceive.

God, give us toughness of mind
not to consent to the destiny of suffering
that comes to far too many
in the world you have created good.

Give us love in action,
that terrifying thing compared to love in dreams,
and help us with such love
to fashion peace between those at war with one another:
peace between neighbors,
peace between races,
peace among the religions,
peace between lovers,
peace between parent and child,
peace between brother and sister,
peace between us and the whole creation, your body,
and all for the sake of our love of you, the loving God,
in whose will is our peace.

Our eyes, seeing these beads of sorrow
begin to weep.
But your heart is big,
so come apart with us and cry with us.

You are a good God
and you love our humankind,
stunning in your unchanging beauty:
life in our passions and passion in our lives.

You Think You Know What Time It Is

You think you know what time it is.
Then say *God is Great.*

For what's the good of wrapping gifts
for friends who have more than enough,
if we haven't opened our loving to God's loving,
if we haven't helped people we do not know,
and have never seen.

You think you know what time it is.
Then say, *God is Good.*

For who imposes upon our heart the regularity of its own beat,
and who poured into our hearts the divine madness of love?
From our own nature we can learn something of
our Maker and Lover, God.

You think you know what time it is.
Then say, *God is Love.*

Even if you've known that unutterable and perfect love
from the beginning of your life.
Say it again.

For the Great God wants us to come together now.

The Good God wants us just for ourselves.

The Loving God wants us to give and to take,
to sing, dance, and be joyful.

Mothering God, Who Gave Us Birth

Mothering God, who gave us birth:
even before we were born,
you held us in your heart.
And when we moved from the womb to the world,
you gave us a mother's arms to cuddle and caress.
And when we could only gurgle our first words,
you gave us a father's funny songs.
And one would hold us until we slept,
and one would cheer us on as we tried to walk,
as we lost our fear.

May it go well with us and our children,
for where love is, you are there.

God of our vision and Joy of our heart:
when something bruised our skin,
you gave us a friend to patch it up.
And when we didn't know what to do,
you gave us a grandmother
to hug us, and listen to us,
a grandfather to let us know that someone was crazy about us,
and knew we would succeed—
so who cared about Ds and Fs?

May it go well with us in every stage of life,
for where love is, you are there.

Eternal Father, strong to save:
when we put away childish things,
and became the adults we longed to be,
you still never let us go,
for you hold us by too many bands.

When we pushed to the limits
in exploring the world and testing its possibilities for us,
you gave us a guide to help us be sure of ourselves.
And when we were stubborn,
and faced our failures,
you gave us a companion with a wider perspective.

May it go well with us and all who hold our community together,
for where love is, you are there.
God of all our beginnings and endings,
when we come to the place of rest,
you will still hide us in your heart,
and shield us in your dwelling-place.
For you alone love humankind.
We will see the light of your presence,
and know the charm of your beauty,
which only song can celebrate.

May it go well with us unto the end and in the end,
for where you are, there is eternal love.

Homo Sapiens to the Great I AM

Homo sapiens to the great I AM:
    From approximately Latitude 42' 52" North, Longitude 78' 52" West.

God, it's a complex world.
    Why are you so silent?
Moral precepts are relative: it's all a matter of choice.
Some prefer chocolate, some vanilla.
So who's to know right from wrong?
    You make it tough for us.

Blessed are the poor in spirit, you say.
    But being rich means feeling good. Doesn't it?

Blessed are the meek, you say.
    But does that mean taking
    whatever tears the heart or lacerates the limb,
    no murmuring allowed, no sulking tolerated?

Blessed are the peacemakers, you say.
    But the orthodoxy is that power grows out the barrel of a gun.
    You make it tough for us.

The great I AM to homo sapiens,
    11:05 EST, USA
    Year of Planet Earth 4.6 billion years

Shout this message!
    Spread it on the Internet:
You've turned against me.
I am more than your idea of God.
    So you wonder why I pay you no regard
        when you go on acting humble,
        trotting out your casual prayers of confession?

Do you think this is what I want on the day of worship?
    Is this the liturgy of the day?
        I will not be silent.

It's not chocolate or vanilla:
    it's kindness or cruelty in every act. Which do you choose?
Your wealth is coming between you and me like a cloud.
You were not ready for the catastrophic climax of a bloody
    century.
You are not fit yet for a century opening with its own obscenities.
Your bombs replace persuasion in dealing with your enemies.
You wrap your pursuit of happiness in a gaudy commercial
    package.
You turn religion into easy support of reigning prejudice.
You take the Word I spoke to you and turn it into an "ism"?
You think only of yourselves.

Turn, turn now, or you'll lose your soul.
Turn, for I am not to be contained, commanded, or possessed.
Turn, and know the final mystery, that I am love.

In this love unbind the chains of all who are chained unjustly.
Free all who are abused!
Share your food with everyone who is hungry.
And make a place of home for those who have no home.

    Then light will shine on you
    light like the dawning sun,
    and you will be quickly healed.

    Then I will help raise up what you have let fall.
    Then I will say to you,
    "This is the day of your salvation."
    Then you will say to me,
    "*This* is the day the Lord has made."

It's Journey's End for Us

If "journeys end in lovers meeting"—
then you have guided us,
Dear Pilgrim God,
to this place as old as Eden,
a home where friends and lovers meet,
easy, familiar, and constant.

Maker of beauty,
help us find delight
in this earthly paradise,
where, standing on earth, we may look at heaven.

Maker of laughter,
you stretch the sky out like a tent
and ride on the clouds,
and the wind becomes your wings.

Come, Fresh Wind of God,
come down,
and teach us what you will for us.
Teach us here the art that opens and heals the heart,
so that intent for justice and wisdom
may become our daily sustenance.

Spirit of God come down,
help us remember
that we are but earth,
unless you kiss us to transform us,
and keep our feet from straying to any deadly path.

Spirit of God, come down
help us know
that we will never here speak heart to heart,
unless your Word is truly spoken and we duly hear,
unless each ask from each what each most wants to give,
and each awake in each what else would never be.

Help us know
that we are refugees
looking to be fed with the only bread from heaven,
wanderers, whose hearts are restless until they repose in you.
It's journey's end for us, Dear Pilgrim God,
for you have surely guided us,
to a place where we may put aside all earthly care,
and learn to feed our minds,
and fire our imaginations,
and free our hearts,
and learn the service to which you call us in the world.

A Moment, Please

Please, a moment with you—
I urge, I urge it of you—
I demand a moment in any place
that will be quietly, only ours.

For any separation from you that I measure,
every abyss of space or time,
is a pit that widens beyond my competence to span.

A moment, please, a space with you that will be quietly, only ours.

"Beauty is the lover's gift." But, ach!
Some evil eye has cheated this jealous lover of that gift.

What is this feverish nonsense that I'm mouthing?
My competence—what is this raggedy thing?
My possessiveness—what is this jaggedy thing, "Demand"?

I own you no more than I own the wind,
Light that shows the way,
Love that knows the heart,
Life within the soul.

Your light is on each step I take.
Your love implacably housed within my heart, and mine in yours.
Your life invigorates my mind and consciousness.

What then could break your encircling of me,
whatever turn your gentle wind away from me?

The moments and spaces, then, that keep us apart—
let them now be glad occasions for incubatory dreams
of how there will be courage on the way
and laughter in the house to which we journey,
Light that shows the way,
Love that knows the heart,
Life within the soul.

And at evening, when I sing the song
of the Land of Promise,
I will be glad for the separations of time and space
that have framed each coming home to you.
So I will fear no other abyss ahead of me again.

ADDRESSING GOD
IN FAITH AND PRAISE

The artist *feels herself* into what she experiences, into the essence of the thing she paints, into what it must be like to *be* the person she depicts or represents.

In turn, we, the observers of her art, *feel ourselves* into what she has painted or provided for us. Art reveals a depth for which words have no expression.

When we come upon something beautiful, then, we can feel ourselves into it and know it intimately. Then it does not simply grasp us. It becomes nearer than our breathing. Since God is the unchangeable beauty in all beauty that we experience, God is therefore the encompassing Spirit, and we (and everything that is) are in God.

It is harder to see that beauty and pain are as inextricably linked as love and pain. If you really want to love—really want to—you are going to have to know hurt also. If you really want to know beauty, the same is also true.

For God, who is beauty and also love is also in every pain.

One Question for God

Do you and I see
    things in different ways? Or are we
        a single eye?

It Might Have Been Otherwise

In the beginning,
    when the earth was barren, with no form of life,
        and a roaring ocean covered it with darkness,
            you created the heavens and the earth.

And, though the universe stretches beyond our imagination,
    you hold it all in the palm of your hand.

You fashioned for us beauty of scene and soul:
    the rising sun each dawn,
    breaking apart the shadows of night—
        each day a gift, a leaping joy,
        in which to live, and love, and do well, and be glad.

It might have been otherwise:
chaos instead of order,
darkness instead of light.
But, wonder upon wonder!
We see the mark that you have placed on this earthly paradise.
Infinitely to the East, infinitely to the West,
we trace the Love that turns the sun and the other stars.

There was a winter wild,
    when the Virgin laid her Babe to rest,
        and the Word that shines on every one
        came into the world.

It might have been otherwise.
As Unmoved Mover,
you might have chosen to be indifferent to our sin and suffering.
You might have had your sport with us,
and teased us with nameless longings
that never can be satisfied.

But, wonder upon wonder!
We see the mark that you have placed on the cross of Christ.
We see the hands of the Savior stretching out,
infinitely to the East, infinitely to the West,
conveying your lovingkindness to all who ask for it.

Another day has come,
   another pause in our lives,
   another occasion to enjoy the pleasant places,
      beauty of scene and soul,
      that you have marked off for us,
   another time to discern
      the shape of the future you have measured out for us,
   another chance to revive old friendships and form new
alliances.

It might have been otherwise.
Change and circumstance might have kept us apart.
Gloom of spirit or chill of weather
might have darkened this day that you have given us.
Ills might have had weight and tears their bitterness.
But, wonder upon wonder!
Here in the open mystery of this day's worship
you look on us again with great compassion.
Here heart can speak to your heart,
and friend can turn for strength to friend.
For you are a good God,
and have made all our ways to lead to you,
and all desires to be unsatisfied, save in you.

Remember Your Baptism and Be Thankful

Beside what water are you standing now?

And because you made
one strong decision to be free,
will you again plunge into the middle flood
through which alone
the way into your future lies,
knowing that only faith—
and sometimes *only* crazy faith—
keeps you from being drowned?

Or are you, like me,
a little hydrophobic when you see
that grey-green swirl before you,
and think, Perhaps I should test the water first,
and dangle my feet a little,
just to test the miracle of grace,
and see a scoopful of water
part before the inset of my biggest toe
(though, if need be, I could endure
a little wetting of doubt
upon the little one).

Help me to jump with you,
my fellow shilly-shallyers at the river side.

Help us to remember, too,
how John once stood beside another water,
and, filled with amazing fear
and hardly yet formed joy,
saw the sudden splash of God-come-into-the-waters.
He loved God then,
and washed God then,
in the liquid history called Jordan.

Help us to know
that only such a plunge
can bring us close to
the God who comes to meet us in our depths.

So Jesus, little Fish of Jordan,
hold our hand and jump with us
into every water of washing,
into every water of terror,
into the icy currents of doubting,
into the swell of every troubling,
into the coolest waters of healing,
into the greenest waters of wonder,
into the reds and blues of splendor.

Help us plunge again
into the fountain of living water.

My God! I'm in the water now,
and floating, gyrating,
exulting, like some rotating
Pentecostal dolphin
in these abundant waters of my baptism.

Not really Episcopal-proper is it?
But first of all it's gleeful,
and close akin (for me thus far) to glory.

Heal Then These Waters

Heal then these waters, Lord, or bring thy flock,
Since these are troubled, to the springing rock.
Henry Vaughan (d. 1695)

We pray for all who feel the overwhelming waters of despair:
for the grieving, deep in their sorrow,
for those who know the loss that is touchstone of despair,
for any who cannot erase a scene of violence from their memory.

Heal then these waters, Lord, or bring thy flock,
Since these are troubled, to the springing rock.

The grieving for whom we pray are troubled,
but you can turn dry rock to water,
and flint to dancing streams.
They are no burden,
so let us carry them to the Rock of Ages,
in whom we find our refuge.

Heal then these waters, Lord, or bring thy flock,
Since these are troubled, to the springing rock.

We lift to you the hurts of Africa,
nurturing mother of the human family,
Africa that takes the heart and grinds it into stone.
Jesus, you yourself were refugee once in Egypt.
Simon of Africa carried your cross to the rocky place called Golgotha
outside the city that you loved like a mother her children.
Do not turn your eyes from Africa
in its present turbulence and struggles to become again a paradise.
Lead the nations of that continent
to a safe place higher than their present turbulence and anarchy,

so Africa may become a beacon
to the violent world beyond its borders,
a nurturer of families,
a transformer of diverse cultures into a just and peaceable society.

Heal then these waters, Lord, or bring thy flock,
Since these are troubled, to the springing rock.

We remember that you have formed on earth
a dwelling-place for your Spirit—
by whatever name we call the assembly of your people.
Yet we have splintered it by our infidelities,
offering froth to people who come asking for living bread,
shortchanging them in holy things,
when they're looking for the truth that is more precious than gold.
What have we to show, we people of your unchanging covenant,
but division and disarray,
as we retreat into the little worlds of our own religious communities?

Heal then these waters, Lord, or bring thy flock,
Since these are troubled, to the springing rock.

For on the rock that is Christ
you have said that you will build a Temple for your Spirit.
So help us learn to dance on that rock,
with ambition that never fails to serve you.
Help us, the people you have chosen
to be servant-priests of your creation
to push away the boundaries that others erect around your church.
Teach us, whenever we break bread,
to remember that you have made us hungry.
Teach us, whenever we drink wine,
to know that you desire only joy for your world.

Not a Bad Combo

This is the story of two men with electric guitars, one with drums, and a large woman with a Tyrolean hat who played a saxophone and sang.

The memorial service for Lilian Williams, the grandmother of Robert, the deputy sexton of our church, was held on a cold day in winter. She was born in 1919, and died of cancer after the New Year. The family gathered at St. Matthew's Church in the village Alachua, Florida, a hundred or more of them. Five of us in church were white.

We were welcomed with evident warmth, and given a funeral fan with which to move the air in the crowded church. We sat in the back row. Five lady missionaries, as they were called, dressed in white, hovered around the grieving family like eager aunts at a family party to see that none fainted and all went well. Two men played electric guitars. One played the drums. A large woman with a Tyrolean hat played a saxophone and sang. It wasn't a bad combo.

For most of the previous two years I had seen Robert only in his role as sexton. He was neat, dressed well, ran a troop for Boy Scouts, and spoke constantly on the phone to his "main woman." That day, I saw him as one of a large and grieving family. His main woman was at his side, sharing his grief.

Robert at one stage came forward to speak in memory of his grandmother. "I have been bad," he said. "And I wondered why God didn't take me before Mother Lillian. Now I know. She was praying for me." A deacon stood up later. "We loved her good. But God loved her best."

This brings me to Tryphaena and Tryphosa. No one has ever heard of them who hasn't read the end of Paul's letter to the Romans. But they are there. We haven't any idea at all who they were, nor any of the others named, like Urban and Stachys. Yet here they are, famed for eternity because Paul once shook hands with them and wrote down their names. For all I know, Tryphaena hovered around her little flock on Sunday like an eager aunt, making sure that all the babies in the place were being cared for. And for all I know, Urban played a flute, and Stachys a tambourine, and Tryphosa played the lyre and sang. It wouldn't have been a bad combo.

Yet through the utterly unknown like these the faith was handed on. Gossamer is fragile, yet it can shine in the sun. And water is unstable, yet it can carry a boat. We properly give praise to saints and sages who crowd the history books, and who have fitting place in stained glass and plastic souvenirs. Tryphaena and Tryphosa: two of the great unheard of. God knows who they were. Just so: God knows who they were.

For People to Whom We Mostly Pay No Mind

Spirit of God,
moving through the heights,
imprint your gracious blessing
on those who make and mend our roads
and let us travel well,
day and night,
in torrent and in snow.

Day and night,
in storm and calm,
be with them all.
Be your own hand on them,
God of the elements,
early and late,
be your own hand on them,
at their rising and at their resting.

Spirit of God,
be near to those who feel paltry, scrubby, and small,
who call and cry out from their hearts for dignity.
Come closer than breathing
to those who cook fast food meals,
clean offices, or make the motel beds,
all faceless workers known to us only by their handiwork.

Day and night,
in season and out,
be with them all.
Be your own breath on them,
Housebuilder God,
early and late,
be your own breath on them,
at their rising and at their resting.

Spirit of God,
shelter of those who plod on year by year
but feel their work has little value,
Be advocate of the poor in the savage race for cheaper labor.
Live with them and be their love.
Bend down from heaven
to raise them from the low esteem
a thoughtless mind assigns to them.
Lift them from any inadequacy they feel.
Be your own heart with them, God,
Champion of their cause,
early and late,
be your own heart with them,
at their rising and at their resting.

Kissing Kin, Not Brusque Competitors

So did they growl at one another,
clambering up the steps to the upper room,
these friends of yours,
quarreling over who's the greatest?

Maids and waiters can't be high and mighty,
so, fulfilling the server's role,
you took a towel and began to wash their feet—
not in a pantomime good for a laugh,
but with the calculus of a goodness
that chooses to live for others,
never seeking the higher place.

Look at us, look on us with patience,
crouched behind names that define our good intentions:
Methodists, yet not so united over sexual issues;
Southern Baptists bumping heads with one another
about submissive women;
Orthodox sniffing at inclusive language;
Lutherans on my right persnickety about dialogue
with Lutherans on my left.
Yet in the upper room you prayed that we might all be one.
Look on us with patience:
us Catholics, sticklers for tradition while priests decline in number,
us Protestants, watching our numbers fall again,
us feminists, turning our back on the patriarchy in which we grew up,
us fundamentalists, insistent that this and this alone is what the Bible says.

Here we all are,
poles apart by any measurement,
too often fierce to seek the higher place,
too little eager to find new ways of understanding
as we growl at one another.

Look on us with blessing,
so many of us here, so different,
but daughters and sons of the living God.
For that is how you see us:
made in your image, all of us,
kissing kin not brusque competitors.
That is how you see us:
born and made, God help us,
to be God's chosen in the world;
guests at your feast,
at which we come to see
how beautiful we are.

"Your kingdom come, your will be done on earth"

So we pray, dear God.
Breathing your own life into us,
you gave us the gift of life, and placed us on this earth to care for it.

Help us, then, create a generous land
where truth and generosity reign.
Preserve our people in justice and honor.
Grant health and integrity to those who bear office among us.

So we pray, dear God.

Help us satisfy the hungry,
not only feed our friends.
Help us warm the homeless,
not only tend our home and garden.
Help us clothe the naked,
not only clothe ourselves.
Help us bind the wounded,
not only remedy our own discomforts.
Help us gather the friendless,
not only gather our own around us.

What a Wonderful World

So, if dragons of revenge are lurking in our soul,
and we just say: *What a wonderful world,*
we find the world we seek.

And if serpents' teeth of malice start gnawing at our bones,
and we just say, *What a wonderful world,*
your love pours down like a summer rain,
and soaks us with fresh joy.

So, if we long to be set free from the prison of a grudging heart,
and we just say: *What a wonderful world,*
Good God! We've found the house of freedom where you live.

And God! With this we're half way to a confession.
And you've come all the way with a forgiveness for us.
And all we said was, *What a wonderful world.*

So, as we find in you the God of forgiving warmth,
the God who yearns for us to come on home,
the God of the transforming touch,
and we just say another time: *What a wonderful world,*
it's like seeing the sun chase shadows away.

If any are here in silent suffering or hidden sorrow,
rising over the pain,
they can say with us: *What a wonderful world.*

If there's an empty space for one of us where a beloved child once was,
or hurt for another, grieving for an absent lover,
putting aside all earthly care
each still can say: *What a wonderful world.*

So, since we all need courage to act with justice and generosity,
and since we want to be drawn to a love
that neither calculates the cost nor keeps the score,
we will from the heart say one more time: *What a wonderful world.*

And when we hear the wisdom of the ancient song:
"Those sowing in tears will reap, and sing, and laugh,"
why, then, we're sitting on top of the pile,
and we can also sing: *What a wonderful world.*

A Jesus Prayer for a Child

Just say, "Jesus, Friend." Say it over and over. Whisper it. Say it when you're tired and weary.

Say it when you're tucked in bed at night. Say it when you're 'real afraid.' Say it when you're feeling bold as brass.

Jesus, Friend,
begin and end,
all I do
for love of you.

Go with us
in all our ways.
Fill our hearts
with loving praise.

Jesus, we love you,
Jesus, we love you.
Teach us to serve you,
To serve you all our days.

Jesus, Friend,
begin and end,
all we do
for love of you.

Go with us
in all our ways.
Guard our soul,
and keep us whole.

Jesus, we love you,
Jesus, we love you.
Teach us to serve you,
To serve you all our days.

SAYING SORRY

The first part of forgiveness has to do with a will to forgive on the part of the one who has been offended. Forgiveness is part of a parcel in which giving and receiving are integral. When I turn towards one who has offended me, I stand in a place of awkward pain. It is awkward, because, since the offense, I have chosen not to deal with this offender. The place is also painful, because I am forced to see in that offender not only what I detest in him (or her)—but what also I have to acknowledge I detest in myself. So the first question in forgiveness is simple: Am I willing to give myself to you—without reserve or hesitation?

The second part of forgiveness has to do with a will to be forgiven on the part of the offender. When I show sorrow for an offense I have caused, my heart will be pierced and I will turn my face towards the one whom I have hurt. Here once again there is a giving and receiving. It is a giving of myself toward the other in repentance and a receiving of the other's response. If it is a response of forgiveness on his part (or hers), then I have received what I utterly did not deserve. It is a grace, pure and simple. It is the mystery of an embrace like no other.

There is a third part to forgiveness. When I pray, "Forgive us our debts, as we also have forgiven our debtors," I am praying not simply to be a forgiving and forgiven person. I am asking that I may be made ready to enter a future where I will not be bound to anything—to any *thing*. I am asking that the effects—even the poisons—of the past may no longer bind, control or damage me. Even more: I am asking that I am asking that I shall therefore from this time become something other than I was. I no longer aim to preserve the personality that I presented to the world before. Old things have really passed away. A new being is in process of formation.

If I Bear My Soul to You

If I bare my soul
   to you, do not shade the light
      from touching my wounds.

But That the Word Be Spoken

The heart can never speak
but that the word be spoken.
Heart of God, you spoke, said, "Let it be"—
and every atom holds the secret of your love.
Every branch and leaf and fruit
reveals some aspect of your glory.
Every rose proclaims a gospel of your beauty.
The world is joyous now because of you.

Why such madness in us—
that we act as if the good life shines for us and only us?
Why such gall—
that we lock ourselves in the room of self,
aliens cut off from the flow of life?
And why such foolishness—
that we let kindness slip from us
like water down a hole?
Why are we afraid to learn
the dangerous new way to live:
that heart can never speak to heart
but that the word "forgive" be spoken.

So teach us the art
that lets the heart rise up from deadness
and lifts the darkness of the soul.
Teach us—as if we had never learned before—
the forgiveness that gives up the urge to get even,
the mercy that will not counter blame with blame.

Life of all life—you are that,
not a God up high on a marble throne,
but here among us, here between us, here within us.

Help us join with you in reconnecting
the shards and fragments of our broken world
into the pattern of the wholeness that you design for us.
Heart of God, you speak. Say, "Let it be"—
and every atom in our being
will share with those we touch the secret of your love.

Learned in Cowdenbeath

For university students of my day two Christian societies offered a welcome and a place of conversation about faith. It was a hard choice, for one took religion very seriously, and the other had all the pretty girls. In these days of heightened alertness to such phrases I feel now an embarrassment in admitting that that was the choice, but it was so. With lower instincts mostly quelled, I joined the serious group.

Every year our society had an evangelistic mission, whether the territory to which we went needed it nor not. One year, our faces transformed as with a glow, we chose Cowdenbeath, in the heart of the coal mining district of central Scotland. It was "red Cowdenbeath" in those days, since its claim to fame or notoriety was to have sent Willie Gallaher to parliament. Willie was then one of the only two communist Members of Parliament in the House of Commons.

Cowdenbeath was a grubby mining town with immensely friendly people in it. They opened their homes to us in hospitality. The miners took us in hard hats and old clothes to the pit face. And the churches took in the students and some professors to preach. We were offering our secret charms to win red Cowdenbeath from its sins.

Some of our charms must have seemed not merely secret but positively esoteric to the simple mining families. G. T. Thomson, our professor of dogmatics, had made name and fame for himself by translating Swiss theologian Karl Barth in English as obscure as the original German. He opened the mission. He stood in the pulpit, wearing his elegant monocle, and uttered a resounding aphorism as the opening sentence of the mission: "There's too much ego in the cosmos."

There probably is, and was. But a miner, sitting beside me, wondered if the reference was to the local dance hall known as Cosmo's. The first thing I learned in Cowdenbeath was that, if you are going to tell people anything about God, keep it simple.

The other thing I learned at Cowdenbeath was harder. I learned what it means to run away.

It was a difficult thing for me to go from door to door as a visiting evangelist. I wasn't ready for the cynics and hecklers. Glaze-eyed apathy is tough for a beginner. On the second or third morning, having received another list of names to call on, I simply took off. I walked the other way, miles into the country, and eventually stopped at a fence and gazed for hours at the cows, feeling disconsolate.

Reflecting now on these early pangs of conscience, I was probably right to catch the next train home, even with a lame excuse. Something in me wiser than my youthful zeal posed the unarticulated question: "What's a nice guy like me doing in a mission like this?

But I remember what it felt like to run away.

I know—and have had plenty of subsequent experiences—what it means to feel a failure in duty and leave others to take over. I also learned that when I blame others now for their outward failures, I am not seeing their inward struggles, let alone their inward victories.

Not all that masquerades as evangelism is worth the effort that goes into it. Televised revivals and similar pious jamborees can do as much harm as good if they are not grounded on the day-to-day life of the people of God in a particular place and congregation. Evangelists who drop by (or intrude on television) to rouse the laggard and rally the ranks may raise the spiritual temperature a few points. We still need the local caring strugglers who live in the place, day in, day out, go to funerals, comfort the sorrowing, visit the sick, or shop for the elderly.

These are the ones who don't run away.

The Image of the Lamb

"Behold, the Lamb of God," the Baptist said.
   Better we had taken a monster out of hell, raw and red,
   as icon of a faith that bids the Lamb of God attend its prayers.

In killing times in Ireland—
   did neither Protestant nor Catholic hear gentle Jesus say,
      "Put down your guns"?

When monk and monarch preached crusade
   against the lands polluted (they said) by Muslim infidels—
   did neither, schooled in ancient faith, hear gentle Jesus say,
      "Put down your sword"?

When Christian guards, off duty from the death camps,
   sang Lutheran chorales in church,
   did they not hear the gentle Jesus say,
      "Put down your xylon gas"?

How, Lamb of God, do we atone the sins of the past?
Or ask forgiveness for offenses done in the name of Christ?
   "Forgiveness to the injured doth belong."

Help us renounce our history of contempt.
Help us turn and ponder the mystery of the Lamb:
   the incapacity to harm.

Armed with this redemptive suffering,
when thugs come looking for another gay to beat,
   we will not stand, consenting.

And when we see the hungry and the homeless poor,
   forgetting self and safety
   we will share the good we have.

And when we hear of women's hopes
    that all may live in peace with one another on the earth,
    we will harmonize with their Magnificat.

And when we find ourselves beside the unjustly treated,
    the wounded and the abused,
    we will take their side,
    and stay, and watch, and work with them
    on the long road of their struggle.

Help us find forgiveness not in mumbled word
    but in pondering the mystery of the Lamb.

Help us live as always willing to forgive,
    to move others from the house of fear to the house of love.

Help us sit before the image of the Lamb,
    and, molded by that gentleness,
    plot to overturn the hatreds of the world
    because you have brought us to live
    beyond the powers and principalities that rule the world.

Who Do We Think We Are?

You drive me up the wall with your religious smarminess,
shoving your "my God is bigger than your God" piety in my
face:
    who do you think you are?

I'm tired of acting humble, you full-fledged misogynist,
I'm not an emotional female; your discomfort around me seems
to amount to hate:
    who do you think you are?

You poor little talkative Christian, why do you talk so much
about Christ
but act so little like him:
    who do you think you are?

Your green eyes give you away: your envy of your friends is a
wound in your soul,
you're eating nothing but your own heart:
    who do you think you are?

You really think it's everyone else these prayers describe, you
sanctimonious fraud,
you can't get off the hook of your own little precious ego:
    who do you think you are?

> *Suddenly an earthquake struck,*
> *and the angel of the Lord came down from heaven,*
> *and rolled away the stone.*

And as suddenly we are shaken,
and something has been altered in the way things run
in the universe,
and the ancient covenant is written anew in every
language of the world.

Who do we think we are?

"We have erred and strayed from thy ways like lost sheep"

Yes, but haven't also you heard?
"The Lord is the eternal God,
Creator of the earth,
who never gets weary or tired of you."

Then, *"We have sinned, we have grievously sinned, and are heartily sorry."*

Yes, but, haven't you also heard:
"I, the Lord, created you.
I have called you by name;
now you belong to me."

We are free at last, and God lives among us:
come to enter into our pain and longing and arrogance,
come to show us that we cannot make it alone,
come to bring us face to face with who we are,
come to let us claim the peace that is the art of living,
come to share the love that is inseparable from service,
come to reaffirm the primacy of the heart.

For everything is made new,
and the old is put away,
and the new creation grows to fullness.

The Evil from Within

We passed the run-down theater on the edge of Soho, loitering by, my two young sons and I. The herald at the door, dressed in pink leather, swathed in beads and languidly proffering tickets, recited her litany with undisguised world-weariness: "C'mon inside. 'Ave an erotic experience." Sin had never seemed sadder, nor Vanity Fair more seedy. The whole thing was a forgery, an illusion, and not the reality of love. Eros must have turned in his grave. But a god like him deserved a parody like her.

Thousands of years earlier another herald recited another litany. "Vanity of vanities," said the preacher, "all is vanity." Good preaching that it was, it was also good news. Good preacher that he was, he pointed to the danger of living the lie—of living with illusion.

All of us have fantasies—sex-differentiated, to be sure, for women and men differ somewhat in their fantasy life. We have fantasies about what we want to cherish or fulfill. Then the illusion gains strength and demands the experience of love or power. So we fill our lives with sometimes bold, sometimes brash, sometimes pathetic semblances of love or power. We create our illusions to sustain us in the struggle of living. I delude myself into thinking that I am different from the common five-eighths of humanity: better (or, if not, at least not as conceited as the others are); closer to God (or if not, at least not as much of a hypocrite as most of the others are).

The simple name of the vice is greed, the sin of illusion. It is the prompt that lets me fool myself that I can grab and get without regard to sex, race, creed, or national origin. It is one of the "evil things" that come from within. It makes us—unclean.

A tornado struck a Florida town one Friday, destroying homes, stores, and a church. Two groups of people left their beds that night: looters and rescuers. Consider the workings of the minds of each. The looter: "What can I get out of this disaster for me? If I grab it before you get it, that's tough luck on you but good for me." If I were a nice looter, I would say the same, but more politely. I would say please and thank you. I would make a bargain with you, sign a treaty with you. But I would still grab and get what I wanted, either of money, things, or sex. But I could keep myself safe in that world only by keeping you out of it. That's the deadliness of it: a world without community.

The rescuers also came. With no expectation of reward or thanks, they came. People needed help. That was it. That was enough. So there is a different way. Another figure, not in Soho but in the sands of Judea, pointed to one who was to come out on the storm of another Friday. John the Baptist, also a herald dressed in leather, called him the lamb of God. Mary had that little lamb, and like other lambs this one was born to be killed. It was tough luck on Jesus that he died, but it was good luck for us. For he invites us to discover the truly erotic experience—which is to strip ourselves of all illusions and find the love that swallows up all greed.

Love like that is a relentless and terrifying thing compared to love in a run-down theater.

Putting Things Together Again

Jesus, son of the carpenter,
stand beside us.
Jesus, worker of wood,
mender of broken things in the village,
take us, rough as we are,
and help us make our star a better place.

Just When We Think We've Got It Right

Just when we think we've got it right,
feet treading firm on the road of our own choosing,
convinced of the high falutin' titles they assign us,
you come like a beggar to our back door,
saying, "This is the way, I am the way."

So fill us with your gracious Spirit
to make us restless until we change,
and let you lead us,
and trust you alone to help.

Just when we think that life has got us down,
and we have nothing of success, or recognition, or possessions, or reward,
you come like a friend, and say,
"Martha, Mike! You are worried and upset about so many things.

So fill us with your gracious Spirit,
and remind us of the one thing necessary:
that you gave us the essential gifts
of faith, and hope, and love.

Just when we think that you're far away,
and not a present hope in time of trouble.
Just when we think you have abandoned us,
you come like a lover who will not let us go.

So fill us with your gracious Spirit,
and teach us to use the time of waiting for you
to discover who we are,
and where we must go,
and what we must do.

Be kind to us, surrounding God, and bless our life.

ADVENTURES

An adventure may be an exciting experience or a bold undertaking. It has within itself the element of hazard, fluke or lucky shot. *Che sera, sera.* By definition, an adventure is something that will happen, but we don't know exactly what. It could be awful; it could be a wonder beyond any expectation. But it will never be dull.

For someone who thinks of God as "the Love that turns the sun and the other stars"—Dante's definition—life will always be adventure. But it won't be hazard, fluke or lucky shot. It will be the adventure marked by the reality that *God* is coming into it—the God you can never pin down, never name and never outguess. Life with this God is turbulent, seductive and draining. It is a waiting for something to happen that is worth waiting for.

This is the God who threw manna into the wilderness like confetti at an Olympian banquet; who put self-righteous Samson into a room with *femme fatale* Delilah; who egged a shepherd boy to take his sling and fell the brass-covered giant; who spoke to Job out of a whirlwind, to Isaiah in a temple so sacred even the guardians of the throne felt naked. This is the God who refused to listen to Moses' mumbling excuses or give happy endings to undeserved suffering. This is the God who sent Daniel, scared to death, into a lion's den, but in the end called him "greatly beloved" and let him talk with angels. This is the God who, when people shrugged their shoulders and said there was no point in waiting for the Messiah any longer, came at the time named Advent, for it is the adventure like no other. This is the God whose name is "I will be what I will be," which means there the future will never be hazard, fluke or luck but a journey where the undisclosed traveler beside us is—my God!—the God we never guessed it would be.

Creator God

Creator God,
Shaper of all beauty
and Sustainer of all that lives:

We thank you for the world in which you have placed us,
fair beyond describing,
and for the world within,
deeper than we can penetrate,
higher than we can climb.

You are God above all, yet in all,
holy beyond imagining, yet friend of folk like us.
To come to you is to find our rest,
to know you is to gain our life,
to see you is the end of all desire,
to serve you is perfect freedom
and everlasting joy.

Another Record for the Guiness Book

Soames should have had a special entry under laziness in the Guiness Book of World Records.

He was—to be charitable—simple. He had been handsome as a young man, they said. I saw a photograph once of a wife and children. By the time I knew him he was a smoky-brown, toothless wonder with a warm, crazy kind of smile. There were medical and other reasons for his sluggish ways. What the medieval theologians called sloth was one of the reasons.

He didn't undress at night before he rolled into his couch in the sitting-room. Not undressing, he said, saved him having to dress in the morning. He was smoky-brown—as was everything else in the room—because he smoked twenty packs of cigarettes a day. Twenty packs. Literally. He would have three going at one time.

Soames had only two front teeth, so he liked cakes. You don't each much with two teeth. But he ate them while they were still in the wrapper. It saved using a dish.

Soames should be pointed to, scathingly, as a particularly good example of the bad habit of sloth. It gives the un-slothful a pinch of righteous joy to bash the sloths of the world, the lazy oafs who sit around while the rest of us do the hard work of the world. The walls of Jericho would not have come tumbling down if some lazy idiots had taken the trouble to put mortar in the cracks.

There is sloth of the body. There is sloth also of the mind. A child, vivaciously inventive at four, becomes an intellectual slug at fourteen. Another, at six, with a treasure house of knowledge to be mined in books, gazes at television a quarter of a day at a time.

There is sloth, too, of the spirit. Do I want to take a step on the journey of the soul to God? Maybe tomorrow.

Soames the sloth had a mother called Allie Mae. When she was dying, Soames was taken by a friend to visit her in the hospital. She had had a stroke. She gave no sign of recognizing anyone, least of all Soames. Soames was instructed by the friend to bend down and whisper something in her ear. He bent down and shouted in a voice that could be heard back at the nurses' station, "Mama! It looks like they scrambled your brains."

With that, Allie Mae gently took his hand, lifted it to her lips, and kissed it. Only a mother like Allie Mae could see the sloth for the son she always took him for.

Always Room for Us

Joiner of the universe
and Makar of all life:*
You molded our bodies when they were formed,
and placed a sense of eternity in our hearts,
perceptible as the air we breathe.

You are always calling us
to follow you into the future
in the strength and faith that you provide.
You invite us constantly to construct anew
in every old and sacred place,
to rephrase and treasure the old
in every fresh discovery we make.

You have told us that unless we become like little children,
unless we take the risk to jump,
unless we let our arms be opened wide,
we will not set foot in your kingdom.

Be around us now
in the adventure and companionship of this day,
as we try new ways to watch and care for others.

Let every room we enter be reminder
that you always will have room for us,
and every door be sign
that if we knock you will open,
and everyone who asks will receive,
and everyone who scarches will find.

Makar is the Scottish word for "Maker." It also means "poet."

A Dump, Far from Paradise

> Observations suggest that the weight of the
> universe lies very near the critical border-
> line between eternal expansion and even-
> tual collapse. . . . Like a ball reaching the
> top of its trajectory, the universe will start its
> inward fall very slowly.
>
> Paul Davies, *The Last Three Minutes.*

The beat-up air conditioner—
it's grinding like an ancient DC-3,
impatient to take off,
lest longer waiting end
the grey asthmatic gasp
of over-strained and undernourished engines.

And here I sit,
surrounded by thirteen square
and five round brown plastic tables,
in turn surrounded by sixty-six (count them)
red and yellow chairs—
a total of two hundred and sixty-four legs.

And on and on I sit,
chewing at time
as if it were a plastic bone.
And now, two minutes later—
it seems like twenty—
still nothing moves.

Three medieval dames with nylon hair
pound in the distance on a Coke machine
reluctant to share its sweetness.
"It's goddam broken,"
the youngest observes to the pudgiest.

Of a sudden, right now,
the whole machinery has stopped.
The beat-up air conditioner wheezes to death.
The Coke machine is sullen, dead.

Just silence.

This is the apogee, the omega point.
The exploding universe has reached at last the top of its trajec-
tory,
and all creation is starting to be sucked
some fourteen billion light years
back into some big, black hole of nothingness,
some measureless point of everythingness.

And here I am, waiting in a dump,
far from paradise,
        but on the first day of the journey back to Genesis.

Footprints

A funny thing happened on the way to the mother house of the Franciscans. Luke was an old-school typographer by trade. During a mission in his London parish he heard a Franciscan monk preach. So he chose, there and then, to live as Francis had counseled: "To follow the teaching and the footprints of our Lord Jesus Christ."

On the way to taking his vows he met Jan. They fell in love, and were married. Settling for ordination as an Anglican priest they came to a slum parish in the city of Edinburgh.

Luke inherited a drab, nineteenth-century church, filled with Victorian knickknacks. Six months before the bishop vowed to close it, Luke restored it to clean simplicity. St. Columba's became a welcoming place to passers-by. Posters of skinny African children adorned the porch wall, and incense from earlier masses seemed like part of the new breath of life.

To be married to a restless ex-Franciscan, living in the slums of a sooty city, took a certain kind of sanctity. Jan had it. She was like a thistle: soft as down, but prickly when she needed to be. She publicly rebelled when her bishop refused to act with charity by barring from the altar a divorced and pregnant girl. If the girl couldn't come to the altar, she wouldn't either.

Three years after they came to the slum, she fell in love again, but not this time with Luke. For four glorious years the slum became closer to a garden of Eden. The more she gave to her lover, the more she found in herself to give. It was as if she had discovered infinity for the first time.

Luke, plodding, loyal, and dependable, uncovered her secret life. He declared it should be ended. That began a pilgrimage of deepening pain for both, ending in flight to an isolated, dreary parish in the wilds of Manitoba. Perhaps distance might cut the bonds she had to her lover. Perhaps a new breath might come in another place. Perhaps an end might come to the anger, jealousy, and depression he continued to feel.

Life is bizarre. Jan tolerated the wilderness for a time. She returned to England. Within months a disabling disease knocked her down, and she, who would have carried any load for any victim, became the load for others to carry. Luke returned from the wilderness to help her carry it. For a year, a month, a week, and a natural day until she died, he bathed her, fed her, and served her.

To forgive. What is that? By ancient reckoning it is one of the spiritual works of mercy. To say, "I'll forgive, but I won't forget," is a kind of incomplete forgiveness. It wouldn't have worked for Luke or for Jan. When we forgive, we still remember the offense, in the sense that we are still aware of it. If we forgive—give the offense away—it no longer has us in its power. We no longer can or choose to use it against the assumed offender.

That is what a one-way ticket home meant for a wandering sometime Franciscan.

We Present Ourselves with Joy

We present ourselves with joy, Creator God,
for looking out, we see this garden of your design
has only life in it.
The earth moves, the lake moves,
and wind like a maniac overleaps the trees.

The sun rises and sets according to your calculation:
Nothing too small a setting for your dance,
nothing too ample for your embrace.

We turn aside like Moses
to see the miracle of every bush lit with your radiance
each path vibrant with your life in it,
galaxies thrown into the void like dandelion seeds.
We present ourselves with joy.

We present ourselves with need,
barely whispering, "Father, forgive."
We are at war within ourselves,
and, ready for a fight,
we've gone to work on others too.

Our scolding words are sharp,
our smiles put salt into the wounds we open.

Don't look at us then look away,
unnerved by our fault and failure,
with coldness in your heart toward us.
We barely whisper, "Father, forgive."

Don't be a dark and hidden God.
Nor let us take your silence as refusal.

Tell us we have no need for fear,
no reason for despair.
Show us that even if we cannot change the past,
cannot unwind the hurt we've done,
you offer us a future, fresh as Eden,
with everything in the world to look forward to.

So let us stand again, like Lazarus,
and wipe the old death from our eyes.
and know we are alive again,
and know the lost are found again,
and know we have come to the merry supper
where you welcome the coming guests,
saying, "Take my bread and eat."

You Don't Have to Like Me to Love Me

Clancy was a thug and a creep. He was an apprentice stonemason, and spent his days chipping letters into tombstones. He had also joined the youth fellowship of our church.

The janitor called me from the fellowship hall. Clancy was in trouble again. Clancy had thrown some flowers down the back stairs. "Not too vile an act," I responded, in hope but fearing worse. The flowers were in a vase, the janitor continued. And Johnny MacMorran had been holding on to them.

It was time to refer the matter to the church. So, remembering that Clancy kept razor blades stitched into his cap—a crude and dangerous weapon—I took the church along to meet Clancy in the robust form of Bill Cochrane, believer and boxer, and especially good when I needed someone to put up his dukes for me.

God has a great sense of timing. When we called at his house, Clancy was in bed, felled by an attack of flu virulent enough to prostrate a horse.

"You've got to give up this violent stuff," Bill growled at Clancy. "You have a choice. Behave and you're in. Screw up and you're out." Here was an insight, good enough for a lifetime. Sin is anyone or anything that keeps a community from living its life to the full.

When we left, Bill grinned. "When I meet people like Clancy," he said, "I remember one of my dad's great phrases: 'You don't have to like me to love me.'" That helps me deal with the Clancies of the world." Bill was right. There are too many screwing up Clancies.

The Gospel of Mark, chapter 13, contains predictions of political unrest, natural disasters, and persecution that will come in the cosmic upheaval just before the return of the Son of man. Jesus gives a terrible warning about what is going to happen. Then, in the most astonishing statement about prayer anywhere in the Bible, he says: "Pray that it may not be in winter."

That is the amazement in what we call amazing grace. You can even ask God to change the date of the end of the world. "Dear God, we know it's an awful world. But don't throw us out into the cold. If you are going to fuss at us—and God knows we deserve it—let it be in the spring. You don't have to like us to love us."

After all, a God like God doesn't deserve a Ross like me. But deserving has nothing to do with it. Everything is freely given by the God who loves us. It is called grace. It is the gift of becoming able to see me as only the most loving of lovers could see me: able to order my life in a way that says no to hurt and yes to affection; no to sadness and yes to joy; no to the lie and yes to the truth; no to the things that keep me under their control and yes to the Spirit that enthralls me with a freedom I had never dreamed of.

A Prayer Incomplete Without the Dance
... or the Song ... or Whatever

I have only
me to offer,
nothing more, but nothing less.
So I bring you
what I can do,
Yours to take and yours to bless.

Bless my living,
and my giving,
and my caring,
and my sharing,
God, so near, so beautiful.

Bless my singing,
and my dancing,
and my loving,
and my touching,
God, my heart is burning for you.

The prayer will be of little help, unless, after saying it, I sing, or dance, or find a place where there is no love, and pour it in.

To a Bubble of Ink at the Foot of a Sheaffer Cartridge

No larger than a tear,
a pearl, a drop of blood,
this bubble of ink is a blue-black well
from which, at my impelling,
words will soon be formed.

I brood upon the infinite possibilities
that swim unformed
in the plastic harbor of this cartridge.

What violent, hurtful, pain-torn words,
what fertilizing, generative sentences
will come to order
when this inky kaleidoscope
is shaken upside down?

One shake more, and I can form
from this reservoir of shapes
words than can end a love affair
(or a hate affair—the choice is mine).
Promote, resign, encourage, dampen, alert, or betray:
out of this fluid
verbs, nouns, and signatures will bring
a memo, page, or plea,
complaining or justified
(the choice is mine).

Here's a pause to reflect.

Will this now diminished drop contain
my last will and testament?
(If so, it better had be brief.)
More surely to the point,
are my last words

really melted together in there,
fluid, until I dry them out one by one
on the washing line
of this yellow legal pad?

Quick, then,
throw the thing away,
even though ink still spatters the inside surface
like rain on a windshield.

Hang the expense.
Into the drawer to hunt
another oil well for my thoughts.

Another pause.

My life is measured out
in a finite number
        of Shaeffer Skrip cartridges.

Shall I See You Smiling?

One day, a million
    stars from here, shall I see you
smiling after love?

What Fool It Was That Invented Kissing

I have a theory that, in order to be human, each of us needs four hugs a day, and you can't accumulate them like snow days or sick days. Each day has its own portion, like the manna in the wilderness. None of the hugs can be kept for tomorrow.

In the story of the prodigal son, much loved by Erasmus, gifted scholar of the Renaissance, we read that when the prodigal came home, his father "clasped him in his arms and kissed him tenderly." Love is like that. That one kiss of welcome expressed the love that makes the world go around. As Erasmus said, "The one who had the greater love did first espy the other."

God is like that. The love that is patient and watches and finally embraces the discreditable is glimpsed early in Hebrew prophecy: "For a brief moment I abandoned you, but with great compassion I will gather you." That was Isaiah. We see that love made flesh in Jesus, who touched the eyes of the blind in Jericho, hugged the leper, and opened his arms to embrace little children. Hugging and kissing are one of the lively virtues.

"I wonder," wrote the satirist Jonathan Swift, "what fool it was that invented kissing." Kissing, surely one of the most common acts of the human race, has been curiously neglected in theology. Theologians are more at ease in discussing love. But kissing is never abstract, like theology.

Kissing, an older encyclopedia of religion ponderously pronounces, "supplies a case of the meeting and interaction of the two complementary primal impulses, hunger and love." More recently, a study of human behavior suggested that in tribal societies it was common for a mother to pre-masticate food for her infant before transferring it direct. That, as the saying goes, makes kissing quite a mouthful, though something seems to have gotten lost in the transfer.

Kissing is rare among semi-civilized peoples, though in higher societies it is both instinctive and fully established. Greek and Latin parents kissed their children in the ancient world, as did brothers and sisters.

David and Jonathan kissed each other as friends. The lover of the Song of Songs kissed "with the kisses of his mouth." Kissing is both the lover's highest art and the traitor's lowest deed. "Give me a thousand kisses," the Latin poet said to his beloved: "To kiss you with so many kisses is enough and more than enough for your mad Catullus." But the kiss that Judas gave to Jesus was a different one, a killing one. When a child is hurt, you kiss the place to make it well. Francis of Assisi cleansed and kissed the ghastly wounds of the lepers in the Lazar house. Sleeping Beauty was awakened with a kiss. Erasmus himself found the kissing in England a most attractive custom: "Wherever you go," he wrote to a friend, "you are received on all hands with kisses; when you take leave, you are dismissed with kisses."

Kissing is the moment when the bond between two persons is confirmed. A kiss, where no affection lives, is violence against the truth. When it gives bodily form to an inner caring, it shows how strong are the bonds of that caring. Kissing comes in many varieties: a touch can be an alternate, and a smile is a kiss by proxy.

Kissing shows most clearly whom and what we revere. An American family, kissing the ground as soon as they landed in Tel Aviv, showed what they reverenced. Pilgrims in Rome for centuries have kissed the toe of the bronze statue of St. Peter, and priests are not likely ever to stop kissing the altar.

Kissing is almost sacramental. It is a real and personal symbol of the life and love that flow from one to the other. It is the common human act that points beyond itself to the love of God who is all in all. Little wonder that the church made it part of its highest worship, naming it the kiss of peace. Little wonder that Jacob Boehme, the Lutheran mystic, spoke of God's approach to the soul as the coming of the Wisdom who "tinctures the dark fire of the soul with her love beams and penetrates the soul with her loving kiss."

A kiss can contain more than a hint of eternity.

He who kisses the joy as it flies
Lives in eternity's sunrise.

That was William Blake, right as always. You can no more demand a permanent kiss than you can bind a butterfly with a rope. The very fleetingness of the kiss points unerringly to its origin in that hot act of love when, at zero moment, temperature a trillion degrees, God made the first big cosmic bang, threw clay into the void, and gave it lovely form—and it was very good.

A God who loves and creates like that quite literally makes the world go around.

A Love That Chooses to Serve and Care

Bless us with a love that chooses to serve and care,
that does not seek to be high and mighty;
a love that can move in color
through fears that are gloomy and foreboding.

Bless us with a unity of spirit,
that we may kiss each other with a fiercer heart,
and show the world
that we are the progeny of your joy.

Lead Us in the Dance

From first to last the Bible is all about bodies. "Thou hast bound bones and veins in me, fastened me flesh." That is Gerard Manley Hopkins, who says, in effect, that I can no more free myself from my physical being than I can stop looking from behind my eyes or hearing from my ears.

God made human beings, moreover, thirsty and hungry. Existence, for most of humanity, isn't feeding like gods on fabled ambrosia or drinking nectar. It is a constant struggle to find food to gulp and water to wash it down.

But then comes the dance.

For when we dance, we become aware that we do not live by bread alone. We dance because we are living beings: living not with our own life only but also with the life of God in us. We dance because we can pass beyond our limits and transcend ourselves. We dance to show we can move from enmity to peace, from loneliness to companionship.

Dancing is the most original of the arts; the generator of religion; the link to the divine through the original dance when the Creator sent stars and planets whirling into the void. The whole universe, when we explore the subatomic world, is engaged in a continual dance of energy and creativity. When we join that cosmic dance, anything we do can become part of the great dance.

Why do we dance? Why should we dance? Because—now we move from the mystery to the practical.

If you fall in love, you don't write, "Dear Sir," or "Dear Madam," to the object of your affection. You write, "Shall I compare thee to a summer's day," or something reasonably close. If you want to express the joy for which God made you, you don't sit up straight, all prim and proper. You begin to dance.

Dancing is the glory of God glimpsed for a moment in a human being fully alive. To watch a dancer is to share in that enlargement, to take part in that coming alive. To be a dancer is to become more than ourselves. To dance is to come closer to God, the original Dancer, the Choreographer of cherubim and seraphim in their most sacred and jubilant moments.

Leader of All Dance

Lord of the Dance,
leader of all dance that is embodied poetry:
Be with all who make music and design the dance
for the enjoyment of your people.
Be with us, shuffle or fly as we may in our dance.
Then with our own joy, close to your eternal beauty,
we will have a glimpse of the perfection
that comes to all who stand before your unveiled glory.
So lead us in the dance, we pray.

Dick and Adele

Dick was the Yank who didn't go home when he could have gone. He was an American airman, based, some years after World War II, at a wartime air base near a village in Scotland called Kirknewton. He was 22. Like lots of his kind, he was far from home and lonely. He didn't see the point of what he was doing. The war was over. He wanted to go home. He dated some of the local girls, went to "the pictures" or to a dance in nearby Edinburgh, filling in the time until he returned stateside. At one of the dances he met Adele. She was bright, bubbling with life, and very attractive. She was a model in a local department store.

I met Adele first in hospital. Just before dawn a call came saying that there was a patient who had been admitted earlier in the evening. It was Adele. The doctor who met me outside the room said that she was terribly injured, badly upset, and she thought she was going to die. She had asked for a pastor, he said, because she wanted to be baptized.

After the dance that evening they had been walking home together. A taxi driver lost control or fell asleep, veered into them, and slammed her against a wall. In the drugged half sleep as she was rolled into the operating room she heard someone call her name. She thought it might have been Jesus. When she awoke from the anesthetic, the paralyzing knowledge came upon her. Her left leg had been amputated from the hip.

Another question mark against the goodness of God. Adele knew only that her life was shattered. What use is a peg-leg model?

Dick stayed with her through that night. He had been unscathed in the accident. Though due to return to the States in six weeks, he applied for a three-month extension. When Adele started to stumble around on her artificial leg, he helped her to go to church. He stood with her and her family when she was baptized.

The extension was over, so he could go home. His responsibility was at an end. But he requested a further extension. By the end of these three months he and Adele were engaged. Within six months more they were married. It was an unforgettable scene. Old St. Giles' in Edinburgh has seen much of the pomp and pageantry of Scotland's history. The model who walked its long aisle that day outshone them all.

Kirknewton was the home from 1786 to 1811 of one William Cameron, minister of the parish. He was also a poet—not a good one, but he had a flair for taking bricks and making them marble, improving the inferior verses of other poets. One that he wrote was sung as part of the wedding service: "Behold, the amazing gift of love the Father hath bestowed." In a sense that no trivial use of the word will mar, the love of God is amazing.

A young American airman, who came for a time to Kirknewton, met a girl and fell in love. In loving her, he came to his fullness. And she, never more complete than when she lost a part of herself, came to her fullness in loving him.

Amazing. Two lovers, born an ocean apart, witnesses to the far-fetched love of God: the love that is patient and kind, and never loses heart, and bides its time, and seeks its chance, and doesn't end.

I Cry to the Distant God

In pain I cry to the distant God—
but who will hear me?
I hurt, and look for a caring God—
but who will hold me?
Are struggles like mine an incident, no more,
on the edge of a bleak, uncaring world?

So what the hell?
What's one more drop in the bowl of human pain?
But it's mine this drop. I hurt.
Or is it mine alone?

Am I not to drink of the cup the Father has given me?

"Suffering, suffering, all is suffering—"
it's a noble truth, they tell.
But show me, show me, distant God,
that somehow what I suffer here
can by some transforming magic
be turned from just plain bloody suffering
to a cup that only a God like you
will share with a guest like me.

Amazing.
The gift of love—
but where's that coming from?
Can a God like you be a God who loves so lavishly?
It makes no earthly sense.

Far-fetched.

And yet—the more we peek and pore,
we find it is far-fetched:
that love come down to earth,
come down to us.

Far-fetched.

And yet—the more we come to think of you as Love,
we find that only those who love can understand
there is no pain that will remain unhealed,
no depth or breadth or height
that love can ever fail to reach.

WE CALL HER
GOD'S GLORY

"The heart has reasons which reason knows nothing of," Blaise Pascal wrote. However logical (and theological) it may be to have a male image of God at the back of the mind, the heart will never be at ease with a God who is more like a father than a mother, more like a judge than a lover, more like a king than a friend. If none are to be kept away from the banquet when "people will come from east and west, from north and south," it will be because the Holy One who then welcomes all will be one in whom all human beings can see and acknowledge the ground and source of their own image, male or female.

So God will be known in women and in men—in both alike and without distinction. So we will look to women and to men for signs of the presence of the Holy, and search for words that let us speak about God in women's ways as well as in men's.

Myra, Maude, and Mandy

Myra wandered, sometimes late at night, leaving her house door open to the world. She liked to sing. The last time I saw her, she sang to me, on key, in the middle of the street at midnight, three verses *a capella* from a song learned in childhood at Sunday school. Do you know how dumb you feel, listening to a crazy woman singing you a song at midnight in the middle of a street? Myra never missed church on Sunday, and usually wore a red flower in her white hair.

Maude sang, too, sometimes, but seriously off-key, and she had trouble with her dentures. They wobbled with her tremolo. Unlike Myra, she was afraid of the night, but she knew help was near when she called the church. I always came. She would invite me in for tea and cookies. Time would slip by, and she would forget why I had come. Do you know how dumb you feel when you are sitting listening to a loose-toothed woman, offering you a party in the middle of the night?

Mandy is legally blind, has grand mal seizures, and when she prays extempore at prayer meeting—which takes God knows what screwing up of her courage to do—she thanks God for all the friends she has around her when the seizures come. She hovers around you, like a troublesome fly you want to swat away.

Myra, Maude, and Mandy and their kind will never be included in any history of the church. Church history is mostly about people who counted for something: the legions of honor who built shrines, devised creeds, died for the faith, and did something to let the glory of God shine in some dark place.

Myra, Maude, and Mandy are numbered rather among the legions of the anonymous simple. They are the weak ones God chooses to shame the strong; the dim ones God chooses to balance and fulfill the bright.

If they have a patron, it should be Simeon the Stylite.

Simeon was the first and most famous of the pillar saints, as they are called. The son of a shepherd, he spent ten years in a monastery in northern Syria. But he found its austerities too diluted, and around 423 of the Common Era he mounted a pillar, and there, on a platform about twelve feet square, he spent the remainder of his life, thirty-six years in all. Despairing of escaping the world horizontally, he tried to escape it vertically.

Every generation stands condemned by the very saints it needs the most. A deaf and blind generation may need the craziness of saints whose attachment to God is as oddly beautiful as singing in the street at midnight. Maybe it takes a madness like Simeon's to bring us even an inch or two closer to God than we were. The world needs them, these saints of one purpose who will one thing. The simple ones bless those who would do them harm, sing songs *a capella*, open doors to the world at midnight, and climb to the top of pillars, the better to see God. The wise, an ancient one told us, will inherit honor. The simple bid us jump into the endless ocean of God. Do you know how dumb you feel if you flinch from getting wet?

Delicate, Fragile Blackbird

Delicate, fragile blackbird that you are,
  your womb three days ago
  gave birth to a woman's life.

Will she one day know
  the pain you carried long before
  the nine months brought their days
  of hope and hurt and waiting
  to an end?

Birth should be a bursting out to life.
Labor should be worthy of the joy
  that a woman is born into the world.

But this begetting was in pain
  as much as the birthing.
No joy was there.
A rape could better be explained.
This begetting was legal—but mad,
  a bundle of emotions,
  a price you paid to bring a lover back.

Maybe if the passing months had brought
  some growing affection and a better knowledge—
  amendment of life takes time—
  but time was never enough to win this game.

A new life is here,
  and all your care, delicate, fragile blackbird
  is centered on that living vote you took.

You lost, that's all.
Don't let her also lose.

You voted with her once, as well as for her.
Let go the price you paid
    to win a love that wasn't worth the pain.
Accept the love you've gained,
    this bundle of emotions at your breast,
    who has her name and life from you.

It's always joy when a woman is born into the world.

For the Light You Let Us See

For the light You let us see in Ruth:
widowed and childless, she abandoned all security
for the sake of love and loyalty to a kinswoman.
And for all unheard of Ruths, who traveled for us into the
unknown:

we praise You, God of the woman
who heard the birds sing in a foreign field,
and join in solidarity with her.

For the light you let us see in Martha and in Mary:
loving Jesus, and keeping close,
they gladly gave their service to him,
gladdened by his own service of them.
And for all the unknowns like them,
patient in listening and learning,
quick in sympathy and tender in care:

we praise you, God of Martha and Mary,
who stood in the heat of the kitchen,
and lived and learned and wiser grew.
We join in solidarity with them.

For the light you let us see in Mother Maria Skobtsova:
working in the pestilent streets of Paris slums,
she saw in every person
the very icon of God.
And in the hell called Ravensbruck,
she saw her Lord come down from the cross
in the blood, the pain, and the broken Jewish hearts
clothed in death camp uniforms.

For all like Mother Maria,
who refuse to separate the heart from the wounds of the world;
and for all women who have worried less about their spiritual life
than whether they fed the hungry and clothed the naked,
we praise you, God of the woman who called herself a torch in the night,
and join in solidarity with her.

For the light you let us see in Mary, Mother of Jesus:
    a girl unheard of beyond her village,
    pledged to a carpenter,
    one with the poor of Israel,
    rooted in the struggles of her people,
    intimate with an angel from beyond the shore of time,:

For all, like Mary,
who have offered their consent to the mysterious plan of God,
who trusted that God would cast down the mighty
and lift up the lowly,
we praise you, God of the woman who sang Magnificat,
and join in solidarity with her.

A Woman Lifted Me Up

A woman lifted me up—
Mary the maid it was—
to let me see the transatlantic liner
ghosting down the slippery Clyde
athwart Dumbarton Rock
en route for New York City.
In darkness every porthole
flashed like lights from a distant village,
but no village floated in such a wonder
as I would never see
except by this glimpse
and at this distance.

A woman lifted me up—
mother's mother it was—
to cradle the crying child
and bandage the wounded knee,
scraped in a fall from a willful bicycle
that would not accommodate a child's imbalance.
A woman lifted me up—
a friend's friend it was—
to cradle the man who had not learned
the vocabulary of pain.
"I will go with you," she said,
"even into hell,
until we come to a place of rest."

A woman lifted me up—
Mary the Maid it was—
gracious Virgin, motherly caresser of the bitter.
Never anyone fled to her protection
and left unaided.

So pray for me, Mary,
pray for all us poor wanderers,
and give us access to the wonder world
that can be our enchanting place of rest.

Clare's Slippers

*The story of Clare is linked for ever with St. Francis. Francis awoke in her a great
vision: not only to transform her very being into the likeness of God, but to serve
the lowest of the low in their need. According to tradition, when Francis received
the stigmata—the marks on his hands and feet, resembling the wounds of Jesus—
she made him a pair of slippers. She speaks:*

See, here is a pair of slippers I have made,
of soft leather, to ease your sore feet.
I ask you only to know of my love.
Many years ago I was in the congregation
when you preached in the great cathedral.
You spoke to my heart.
I came to you, to speak to you about God,
and how I might serve him.
And you encouraged me.
And I knew there would be no turning back for me.
You had your Franciscans,
and I could have my Clares.
We were as poor as your beloved field mice.
Poor Clares!
And this poor Clare cut off one lock of her hair
when I took the vow of poverty.
I held on to nothing—not even my curls!
I wish there were world enough and time enough
to do all I have to do,
all I want to do.
My heart is full.

My name is Clare, I only ask to be
a sign of God's accepting care and grace;
a pointer to the love that gently works
in lowly places and mysterious ways.

The love that turns the sun and all the stars
alone can warm these stony hearts of ours.

You bade me share with God my very being.
You helped me find another way to see.
A larger beauty than I ever knew
came suddenly to me that very day.

In God's good time I heard God's call to me,
and as God's servant I was wholly free.
I thank you, God, for this so gentle friend,
mirth-loving troubadour of joyfulness.
Had we another life to live,
I still would love you, Francis, as I do.
We plumbed the deepest mystery of love—
God's love, that bound my inmost soul to you.

A JOURNEY
ONE STAGE FURTHER

At the end of his eloquent protest against death Paul the Apostle says, "Therefore stand firm, because you know. . . ." But what do we know about death? That it may be "an endless night to sleep through" as a doleful poet of Rome once said? Or is it "the goal of our career and the necessary object of our aim," as Montaigne with a little more cheer concluded? Or, in the words St. Augustine said, is it the moment when the soul crosses over from this world to the other?

It matters a lot who is right. It is a matter of taking a bet: that death is the unique point between time and timelessness when we give up our earthborn limits and allow the Mystery we name as God to take possession of our spirits. It is the opposite of resignation:

> it means accepting that death is not the final limit, but the point at which we allow God to put a seal on our personal life and say, "Good for you." It will be good for you. That's the bet. For God never stands far off. So though grief may grasp us for a time, even at the grave we may stand firm and make our song: Alleluia, Alleluia, Alleluia.

You Were There

Infinitely caring God,
when pain and puzzle come to us,
a voice sounds in our ear:
Give up the foolishness.
No blood flows in the veins of God.

And the ancient singer said,
"The best fate would be not to be born,
not to see the rays of the sun."

And Job cried, "Why, why, why?"
And the dogs of pain were ravenous to eat his very soul.

But you were there:
in and under and with the pain.

And Jesus cried, "Why? My God,
why have you abandoned me?
Feeling the nails in his assaulted body,
his sweat became great dollops of blood.

But you were there:
in and under and with the pain.

We remember all in pain:
victims of human bestiality,
used sexually without consent,
tortured and humiliated,
whose misery mocks our faith that God is good.

But you are there:
in and under and with the pain.

We remember:
those whose lives will be short,
whose months and days are numbered;
plain worn out folk,
distraught by death, or suicide, or accident;
the lonely, who long for someone's love;
the pressured, who fear they are going to crack.

When we dare to look, you are still there:
in and under and with the pain.

We remember those who are hurting by our exclusion of them,
all who feel kept out by our manner
towards those who are "not like us."

Help us dare to look, to see you there:
in and under and with the pain.

You have told us,
"My people, you are my witnesses,
and my chosen servant."

So if we are, then you are God.
And if we are not,
it is as though you are not God.

As we work out through these prayers
a pattern of how to love and how to care,
help us hear the cry of innocence arising from the heart of evil.
Feeling the nails in their assaulted bodies,
help us enter the pain of those in grief or bereavement
alert, listening, reaching out, and touching.

For you are always there:
in and under and with the pain.

That You Remember Me

When Bill Arnold was on the staff of a church in Louisville, he received a call at two in the morning. The caller was in agitation. "On the day of judgment," she began, "are those who have died first judged before those who died after them?"

Still waking from sleep, Bill asked her why she called him about the question. Particularly, why him? "Well," she said, "your name was the first on the Yellow Pages under clergy."

Her son, she said, had never made anything of his life. At school he had been arrested by the police many times. He drank too much, was hooked on drugs, and had got a girl pregnant. So he joined the army and was sent to Vietnam. On a night maneuver he had been ambushed and killed. "But on the day of judgment," she said, "I want to speak a good word for him."

To pray for the living and the dead was one of the seven spiritual works of mercy by medieval reckoning. If the evidence in early texts is anything to go by, Christians have been praying for the living and the dead as long as they have been doing anything.

A fourth century bishop of Jerusalem stated in his instructions to his priests that the dead were to be regularly commemorated in the Sunday prayers of the church. One of these prayers, sung at the time of Eucharist, goes: "Then, we remember those who have fallen asleep before us, because we believe that those souls benefit very greatly from our prayers."

In loving and colorful ways the living remembered the dead: "We pray . . . for the sons of Gregory who are laid in this village." ". . . for the poor woman and her two sons." ". . . for those who have held up the orphans and widows, Emir Matthew and Emir Hassan." ". . . . for all them that in a true faith departed from this world, of whom our Lord alone knows the names."

To pray for the living and the dead is to envelope them in our love. More to the point, it is to declare our confidence that the God to whom we pray also envelopes them, but in a larger love than ours.

To pray for the dead is to declare our hope—in the words of a canny old Scot—that "they do not cease to live whom God does not cease to love."

The living may be in a different place, but they are still close to the dead for whom they pray. Because the dead are close to us, we no longer belong completely to this world. Because we are close to the dead, the dead still belong to our history. *That you remember me.* That is the other side of praying for the dead. We remember the dead as we pray; but we are also remembered by them. True remembering means that there is a good word that always can be spoken: about the poor village woman and her sons; about Emir Matthew and Emir Hassan, whoever they were; and about the Louisville woman and her son. They still belong to our history. They remember us. We still belong to them.

God of Life

God of life,
when I came into this world,
I brought nothing with me.
When I leave it,
I'll take nothing out.

So much for my beginning,
so much for my end.
Why, then, need I fuss,
or worry yet awhile?
Just give me, in the time between,
a taste of another life—
something eternal,
a sip of what might be
far beyond my imagining.

Help me to see that, when I'm dead,
the earth I didn't love enough
will hold me closer than a lover.
Let me trust that what I leave behind
is not a body moldering under grass
or turned to ash in fire
but fragrance of a life that still gives joy to some,
or pleasure to a friend who still is near,
or memory that still gives laughter,
part, perhaps, of someone's very being,
closer to those I loved than ever,
and nudge to the forgetful that I still belong.

Help me see that, though my rendezvous with death is certain,
I haven't thrown away my soul—not yet.

I haven't thrown away my loves—not ever these.
I keep the faith that I am loved,
still loved.
This thought *will* bring my heart relief:
I will not die in solitariness,
for friends and lovers will remember me
as I remember them.

The dead we call the dead—
they will not cease to live:
For you never cease to love.
In you there is no edge between the living and the dead.
All are one in your love,
near terrifying in its intensity.
All will finally meet
in a place beyond our human touch or sight.
All will grow from limitation
toward the true perfection,
which is to see you face to face.

This Little Light

Liz was my age. I knew her well, and had much affection for her as a Benedictine, a teacher, a librarian, and an authentic and deeply caring human being. Had she not been so caring that awful day, the accident might never have occurred. But it did, and Liz died, and (to quote a poet who also grieved, and to speak for all who loved Liz,) "Oh, the difference to me."

Before the accident, Liz had arranged that my class at the seminary should come to worship at evening prayer with the Benedictines at St. Gertrude's. We had wanted to pray with the community as they sang the office, using Gregorian chant. I assumed the proposed visit was canceled, but, true to Benedictine hospitality, the sisters urged us even more strongly to come. It would be a good remembrance of Liz. So we came.

The class of which Queenie was a member had been in open conflict: racial, theological, and social burrs chafed under black, white, and brown saddles. Queenie—true to her regal name—took control with all the gentleness of a lamb. She led us in worship one day, and it was a sign that armistice, if not peace, had come, when all the voices, cracked and canorous alike, united in a song that became almost a theme for the class.

"Among my people," Queenie explained, "this is a song we love to sing when we 'become church.' It says there's something in me that's got to come out and lighten someone's night." So she taught us to sing, and to clap, and to sway:

This little light of mine,
I'm going to let it shine:
Let it shine, let it shine, let it shine.

The evening we came to St. Gertrude's the sisters welcomed us, and the talk turned to Liz, and we shared a common grief again, and then it was time to pray. So we prayed, and the Gregorian chant, solemn, flowing, and free, touched something deep in our core. Then it was time to go.

I don't know what crazy impulse prompted the next suggestion. Thanks were due to our friends. I simply asked Queenie to put our gratitude into words.

"We've learned a song," she explained, "and it comes out of my heritage. But you've sung for us, and we've sung with you. We'd like to sing it for you, and we'd like for you to sing it with us. It's a song that says there's something in me that's got to come out and lighten someone's darkness."

So we sang.

This little light of mine,
I'm going to let it shine:
Let it shine, let it shine, let it shine.

And the blacks and the whites of the class sang, and the conflict was ended; and the Catholics and the Baptists and the Presbyterians sang, and peace was among them; and the living and the dead sang, and you knew that only a veil as thin as air now separated them. And Liz would have loved it.

We See, But. . . .

We see, but we don't believe what our eyes are telling us.
There's more we need to see: more light than comes through
the window frame.
We understand what our minds conceive.
There's more we need to know: for if by knowledge alone
we come to you,
then only the witty and wise will know the way.

To have a vision of who we are and who you are for us
we need . . .
the light that comes from you, letting the night shine like day.

For your word is a lamp for every step we take,
a light that shows the verge of every path we walk.

So even though we trudge in valleys that reek of death,
nothing will disturb, no terror frighten us,
for you turn all darkness around us into light,
and conquer death with life.

You've called us to be the light of the world.
But do you really mean us to drench the world
with the splendor of God?
A deal:
It won't be our light anyway, but yours.
Flicker it may, but fail it never will,
for the light and love and power in us are yours,
given to show the world a better way,
put broken things together again,
and raise the low and lonely up to God.

A Dance in Paradise

This is a story about a long walk into the heart of the rice paddies near Kottayam in South India.

At Father Alexander's invitation I went with him to the rice paddies near Kottayam. The mother of his sexton had died, and he thought I would like to attend the last rites. At the road's end, it was a long walk in the burning sun into the heart of the paddies.

From a distance we could make out the primitive settlement. As we approached, the thirty or so who formed the old woman's family came forward shyly to greet us. She lay, swathed with a cotton sheet, in a coffin her son had crafted for her.

Father Alexander chanted the prayers of the church. When the service was over, he invited me to say a few words, which he would translate. I mumbled something about the new growth in the rice fields, and spoke about the God who is always calling us into a life that is more than life. Then the sons lifted the coffin, and carrying the load in turns, walked along the earthen wall through the paddies, singing lyrics about the sun not harming by day nor the moon by night.

When we reached the road, it was so hot that I asked, discreetly, how much further it was to the churchyard. "Two furlongs," came the reply. I cursed my fragile memory from school days. Was it eight miles to the furlong or eight furlongs to the mile? It was the latter, as it turned out, and we reached the church and stood around the hole that had been dug for the burial.

With more prayers and lyrics about rising to new life, we laid the old woman in the soil of India: "All of us go down to the dust; yet even at the grave we make our song: Alleluia, alleluia, alleluia. . . . May your portion be peace, and your rest with the Redeemer be this day in paradise."

Incredible. Here was I, richer than King Croesus in comparison with her, with a degree in a subject she wouldn't have known how to spell. Yet here was she, resting with her Redeemer in paradise, seeing and hearing what prophets and sages have longed to see.

Two Texan friends, Mac and Anne Turnage, have come through their own tough times. He was born with a back deformity that gives him a hump; she came through difficult cancer years ago. Mac is the least deformed in character of any I know, and Anne healthier in spirit than most. Both are writers. They have written into their wills that at their funeral they want to have a paragraph or two out of their own books read: "We'd like to have the last word," they explained. Then, they want all their friends to go somewhere special after the service and have a party. Everyone connects Mac and Anne with parties. Finally, they want to install a simple plaque in a janitor's closet in their church. "What on earth for?" I asked. "We want someone fifty years later to come across it and say, 'Who on earth were Mac and Anne Turnage? And why on earth is their memorial in this dump?"

What they will be is more important by far than what they ever were: they will be in paradise somewhere with the Redeemer, and a janitor's wife from India will join them in one of the dances.

Think of the Dead with Kindness

We think of the dead with kindness
and honor the dead we loved for a while:
for they are your friends,
and we share your joy in them.

They are one with you,
for they welcomed you
as guest into their hearts.

You are one with them.
For you have found in them a place to dwell.

You are their God, they your people.

You brought them out of sorrow.
The sun shall not harm them by day,
nor the moon by night.
For you have brought them to the place
where torment and death shall never touch them.

When they passed through trial and pain,
you consoled them with your love.

You have set them free,
so now they can walk with heads held high,
their mourning turned to dancing.

Truck One In

Only twice in my life have I been taken to hospital by ambulance. I was a bit disappointed both times that there were no sirens or flashing lights: but for scarlet fever at age five and a swoon at age forty, that would have been overdoing it. So I have little knowledge of what it means to be sick and have visitors around me. But I have a lot of what the graceless jargon refers to as "hands-on experience" when it comes to visiting the sick. The wise ones of old called that a corporal work of mercy.

This brings Nancy into the picture. Her picture is still in our room. A red-headed, vivacious, and endlessly entertaining companion, she was a mimic without peer, a storyteller, and a teacher of the old school, who was guided by three pedagogical tools: love the children, let them grow, work them hard. She did all three better than anyone.

The photograph shows Nancy with a forsythia bush behind her. It was Spring that day, warm with all the fragrances of April in Virginia, when she told us that she would not live to see the forsythia bloom again. We had known she was ill, and had struggled against cancer for ten years.

She knew she was facing death. So in the new hospital to which she was taken the following Spring, she asked one day for a chaplain. She wanted to talk about her death. No chaplain was available, she was informed. Her answer came with a snort worthy of a Byzantine queen: "Then truck one in."

They did truck one in, but he was hardly dry behind the canonicals. He neatly sidestepped her questions about death. She augustly banished him from her sight. "Go play with your marbles elsewhere," she intoned. "I mean business."

Her business was dying, and she knew it. She said on one visit: "I've discovered the meaning of the medieval phrase, 'To make a good death.' It means I cannot die in peace unless those who love me give me permission to die. If they hold on, they are denying the thing that is most real in the world to me right now."

She asked me to help her to die. She could drink only liquids. But if I could remove the powder from the capsules—"Only thirty-two are necessary," she said—and add water to it, she could drink it. But I was needed to help.

Only those who have made the journey with the terminally ill know how rocky the road can be. She wanted to die. The pain was too much. It was time. She asked me to say farewell. She needed the last draught.

I said I needed to pray about it first.

I left the house quickly and drove at seriously illegal speeds to the church I would otherwise have been in. It was just time for holy communion. The people were coming forward, old and young, black and white, the lame, the maimed, and the blind. They were a grubby lot. Of a sudden I felt something so real you could smell it, touch it, taste it. "Sanctify us," the priest prayed, "and at the last bring us with all your saints into the joy of your eternal kingdom." Sanctify us. Make this grubby lot—saints.

I could think only of Nancy, bald and scarred. She was a chrysalis saint, and the baldness, the stigmata on her body from the surgeon's knife, and the weakness of her body were but the form she had assumed before she came to her perfect form in that eternal kingdom of which the rest of us grubby saints had sung about off key. Grubby? And one of them was carrying death.

I went back and told her about the song we had sung off key. She smiled. She relieved me of the need to help her die. She would do this on her own. I suspect by then she was hearing another song. She longed to go and hear it up close.

KNOTTING

Take me to you, imprison me, for I,
    Except you shall enthrall me, never shall be
free,
    Nor ever chaste, except you ravish me.
John Donne

When you finish the work, you knot the threads to keep them from unraveling. I'm not sure I want to do that yet. At least, not every thread. I want to leave some hanging. Prayer and story-telling are best when they leave something dangling; when they have the capacity to be heard again with new or altered meaning. A prayer repeated like a formula will never be more than that—a formula. And prayer in public places is too often as formulaic as the disembodied voice that announces gate changes in an airport. Likewise, stories told in private places are always better when we hear them with an unfamiliar nuance or adornment; when they are different every time they are told.

I find it very hard to pray.

This may seem an odd confession when I have provided a book with many prayers. It is true nonetheless.

My mother taught me to pray thus when I was three or four:

Gentle Jesus, meek and mild,
Look upon a little child.
Pity my simplicity,
Suffer me to come to thee.
God bless . . . .

A laundry list of prayers for others followed, from grandparents to starving Armenians.

When I became a man, unlike the apostle Paul, at least in praying I did not put away childish things. I still prayed the formulaic prayer, now in more sophisticated fashion: "Fulfil now, O Lord, the desires and petitions of thy servants." A work order of requests followed, from grandchildren to starving Ethiopians.

Prayer and Beauty

In wondering about how to pray, I changed when I discovered three things.

The first is the connection between prayer and beauty. I put away childish things when I found what it means to welcome as a lover the God who, in St Augustine's words, is "Beauty Unchangeable." John Donne had the perfect but stunning image for this: we find our true freedom when we are ravished—emotionally overwhelmed—by the God whom we do not want ever to leave because we keep hearing a voice, "Don't go yet, don't go yet."

It became much easier then for me to brood, as in the presence of God, while listening to the slow movement from Mahler's Fifth Symphony. A trumpet solo by Miles Davis lifted my heart up much more than reciting *sotto voce* "Glory to God in the highest." To gaze at Picasso's "Guernica" and grieve, as in the presence of God, became for me a better way of confessing sin than saying, "Almighty and most merciful Father, we have erred and strayed from thy ways like lost sheep." And if a scalawag like Robert Burns could look in ecstasy at a flower, why could I not join him and pray joyfully, as in the presence of God, and sing like him? And what a song it was:

> Bonny wee thing! canny wee thing!
> Lovely wee thing! wert thou mine,
> I wad wear thee in my bosom,
> Lest my jewel I should tine [lose].

Religious poetry from the Song of Songs through Julian of Norwich (c. 1342-c.1416) to Denise Levertov (1923-1997) has typically found a center in what Levertov herself called "the oneing with the Godhead." Prayer, when I came to see things this way, is not my approach to God but God's approach to me with the passion of a lover. Jalal al-Din Rumi (1207-1273) writes thus of the divine foreplay:

> Lord of Beauty, Lord of Grace,
> Enter my soul
> like one who enters a garden in bloom.

This sense of being ravished by the God who is beauty, and who is known (or hidden) in all beauty, is a thread that binds Judaism, Christianity, and Islam—the Abrahamic families of faith. The Sufi philosopher, Ibn al-Arabi (1165-1240) writes:

My heart holds within it every form,
   it contains a pasture for gazelles,
   a monastery for Christian monks.
There is a temple for idol worshipers,
   a holy shrine for pilgrims;
There is the table of the Torah,
   and the book of the Qur'an.
I follow the religion of Love
   and go whichever way his camel leads me.
This is the true faith;
This is the true religion.

The entrance of the divine Lover who is unchanging Beauty. My mother never thought of it this way. But perhaps calling on "Gentle Jesus" was the first "paint by number" attempt that could bring me to al-Arabi's true faith and true religion.

Prayer and Love

The second change in wondering about how to pray came when I found the related bond between prayer and love. I do not think of love here in a plastic but in a perturbing way. Dostoevsky (here as always) helped me: "Love in action," Father Zossima said in *The Brothers Karamazov*, "is a hard and terrifying thing compared to love in dreams."

Hard and terrifying: the more intense love becomes, the more we shrink from its intensity. Moses did not tremble on Mount Sinai because he saw a bush in flames without being consumed. He must have seen many bush fires before. He trembled because he sensed there and at that moment and in that place he was in the presence of "the Love that turns the sun and the other stars," to use Dante's vivid phrase.

That may be the reason it is hard for people like me to pray: because if prayer is really a meeting with God, then we are coming close to the searing heat of a love that billions of years ago shaped a formless emptiness into a cosmos and said, "Yes," and called it good. No wonder Moses took his sandals off. For it means that when I pray, I do so not as the mumbler of a sacred formula, but as a lover who must come to know the vast scope and frightening demands of authentic love. I must pray as a *lover:* as a lover of all things quirky, quaint and curious. The universe, from quasars to quarks, is therefore the scope of my prayers. I pray as a lover, therefore, of all things grand, majestic, tiny and timid. A lover who feels the urge to try to put the broken pieces in my part of the world together again. A lover who says, considering the poor, the waif, the offended against, the dreary, the weary and the afflicted: "I hold thee by too many bands and will not let thee go." That is the scope of my praying.

When I pray (I came slowly to see), I therefore pray as a person and not just as an individual. A "person" may be an individual, but is always more than an individual. An individual is a skin-encapsulated ego, a self-balancing biped, a creature defined more or less by the limits of height, weight, sex, moment in history, and social security number. *As an individual,* I am me and not you. I live in this time and not another. *As a person,* I am (in ways I cannot even imagine) bound up with mine—with my family, my friends; with the things turn me on or lift me up. Similarly, I can know *you* only as I know yours: your folk, your connections, your yearnings. If you are sick, preparing for an examination, or about to jump off a cliff attached to a hang glider, I will, if I care about you, think about you intentionally as in the presence of God. I will link my presence to you with your presence to me, with God's presence to us both. This is what it means (for me) to pray with and for other people.

When I pray with other people, I share in their personhood and they with mine. In so doing we become a community and not just an aggregation of individuals. When we pray for other people, we commit ourselves to taking a share in their personal lives, in all that happens to them. "If you prick us," Shylock asked, "do we not bleed?" Indeed we do: for if someone in the community of praying people is hurt, or someone known to them is hurt, the whole body is hurt. "If one member suffers," to use Paul's language, "all suffer together with it" (1 Cor. 12:26). So we pray constantly for one another when we remember that I am bound up with you and you with me.

Prayer and Silence

The third change in my wondering how to pray came when I discovered silence.

Henri Nouwen wrote that driving through Los Angeles gave him the strange sensation of driving through a huge dictionary. All around him were words on signs, posters and directions. The business of the world is conducted by words. I myself fell in love with words when "Teddy" Albert taught me at school that it is through writing, reading, speaking or singing words we discover who we are and who we are not. He loved Shakespeare's sonnets, Addison's essays, and Hardy's novels. He encouraged me to memorize the whole of the *Oxford Book of Modern Verse*. He opened a whole new world for me.

My life from that time has been dominated by words. I have been a pastor, a professor, and a writer. I came to realize, however, that, if truth be told, saying prayers can be a barrier to coming to know, let alone to love God. Just as there are some chatty people whose constant chattiness raises a semi-permeable barrier and keeps us from knowing them, so we can rattle off our prayers and blithely assume that God likes it that way.

Intimacy comes not only from words—even words like "I love you"—but from silence. You know you've got intimately close to someone you love when you don't need to keep being a chatterbox. You simply sit or lie or walk, being quiet. But this silence is not empty. It is a silence of growth and knowledge and discovery.

Rumi in one of his Discourses talks about this entrance into silence when we pray:

> We know then that the "soul" of prayer is not only its external form but also a state of total absorption and unconsciousness during which all these external forms, for which there is no room, remain outside.[1]

A state of total absorption: this is the "oneing with the Godhead" of which Levertov wrote. In the Divine Liturgy of Eastern Orthodoxy the celebrants stand before the altar and sing, for the congregation, the Cherubic Hymn: "Let us, who mystically represent the cherubim, now lay aside all earthly cares." When we pray we lay aside *all* earthly cares—the tumult, huckstering and dins that assault us throughout the day and echo in our dreams at night. But in prayer we can envelop ourselves in a silence that becomes the perfect expression of our intimacy with God.

So I Can't Stop Praying

It is a curious circle, this matter of praying. It has twists and turns of many kinds, but as you follow the path it takes, you come back to the beginning and discover it as if for the first time. It is a kind of second naivete, the time to accept the formulas that withered away only now to produce new fruits and flowers.

So I discover that, hard though it is for me to pray, I can't stop. I can't stop any more than a lover can stop saying to the beloved, "I love you." Same old formula, sure. But, then, it is the same old love, now revealed to be terrifying in its intensity.

So my mother, God bless her Calvinist soul, deserves some credit. She did her best: and look where the first steps led me. George MacLeod, founder and leader of the Iona Community in Scotland, deserves his portion of thanks. I am sure you can hear something of him echoing in the prayers of this book. I stood beside George one evening in the refectory of Iona Abbey when he called on the group to be quiet for the grace. I closed my eyes. At the "Amen," George snapped: "What were you thinking of when we were praying just now?" I gulped and said, "Mmh, nothing in particular." "That's the trouble with our prayers," George said. "We usually—like you—have nothing in particular in mind when we are praying." For George, committed socialist that he was, that meant it is empty prayer when we include the poor and oppressed in our prayers if we do nothing to follow the prayer by way of social and political action. To pray for friends by name is incomplete unless the prayer is followed by an "Amen" in the form of telephone call, visit, or letter. I think George would recognize some of his own tones in the prayers I have provided in this book, and I think he would still ask me what I plan to do as a result of praying this way.

I thank Jeremy Burdge, MD, for calling my bluff when I promised or the umpteenth time that I would consider putting my prayers down in print. Many of the prayers in this book were written for the ecumenical and interfaith Sunday assembly of the Chautauqua Institution from the years 1990 to 1999. Jeremy gave me the push I needed, with further extraordinarily generous promise of help, to put the threads of this work together.

I thank Charles Mahon, editor of the *Catholic Virginian*, for permission to use material from some of my columns in that paper. Charlie gave me a vehicle for saying some of the things I wanted to say, and I remain grateful to him.

To have a copy editor of the skill of Dr. Lauren de la Vars will make any text better than what emerges from the computer. I thank also Judith Olsen Gregory, president of the Chautauqua Center for the Visual Arts, for adorning the text with her inimitable sense of beauty. Others have encouraged and supported: notably Penny Austin, who knows well how to turn a dreary day into merry party and a drab place into home of welcome and joy. And I thank Cynthia Campbell, president of McCormick Theological Seminary, for reading the early version of the book and appraising it with the skill that only a maker of words such as she possesses.

To the congregations at the Chautauqua Institution who first heard these prayers I give my enduring thanks. No one—neither priest, pastor nor president of the assembly—ever prays *to* a congregation. The best she can do (or he) is to pray what the congregation would pray were it (the congregation) fashioned out of many into a single voice. The praying person prays with and for a people who need that one voice, but need it as a group of travelers need a ferry to get from this to another place. The ferry may be ugly or newly painted, and the praying person may be gifted or stumbling. Helping people get there is the task. I think of myself in these prayers and stories as just a ferryman, a kind of spiritual Charon. To revert to the image that is the title of the book, I am just the putter together of threads. If the material produced by these threads can be used, or worn, or enjoyed for a time, that will be enough.

Ross Mackenzie
Chautauqua Institution

NOTE

1. In *Signs of the Unseen: The Discourses of Jalaluddin Rumi*, p. 13, introduction and translation by W. M. Thackston, Jr. Putney, Vermont: Threshold Books, 1994.